ICONS
AND
IDIOTS

ICONS
AND
IDIOTS

STRAIGHT TALK ON LEADERSHIP

BOB LUTZ

PORTFOLIO / PENGUIN

PORTFOLIO / PENGUIN
Published by the Penguin Group
Penguin Group (USA) Inc., 375 Hudson Street,
New York, New York 10014, USA

USA | Canada | UK | Ireland | Australia | New Zealand | India | South Africa | China

Penguin Books Ltd, Registered Offices: 80 Strand, London WC2R 0RL, England
For more information about the Penguin Group visit penguin.com

LIBRARY OF CONGRESS CATALOGING-IN-PUBLICATION DATA

Lutz, Robert A.
  Icons and idiots : straight talk on leadership / Bob Lutz.
    pages cm
  Includes index.
  ISBN 978-1-59184-604-8
  1. Leadership—Case studies. 2. Automobile industry and trade—
Management—Case studies. 3. Lutz, Robert A. I. Title.
  HD57.7.L875 2013
  658.4'092—dc23   2013006817

Printed in the United States of America
10 9 8 7 6 5 4 3 2 1

Book design by Pauline Neuwirth

Penguin is committed to publishing works of quality and integrity. In that spirit,
we are proud to offer this book to our readers; however, the story, the experi-
ences, and the words are the author's alone.

To Zoe, Sophie, Molly, Ziggy, Pumpkin, and little Misha,
all dogs and cats of class who bring comfort and joy.

CONTENTS

ICONS
AND
IDIOTS

PREFACE

THIS BOOK is about leaders and leadership. No "recipes" are offered; it's a compendium from my more than sixty years of observation while basking in the glow of inspirational leaders, trying my utmost to validate my employment to the tough, sometimes irrational ones, and marveling at the multifaceted, ever-shifting personalities of some of the quirky ones, wondering, at times, how they ever achieved their lofty positions.

Looking back with the rosy glow of history, I have attempted to analyze what made the great ones successful at what they did, and why some of what I perceived, at the time, to be crazy, almost counterproductive behavior had to be cast aside in the overall assessment of their effectiveness. It was like distracting "snow" in a television program of important consequence.

We'll examine past bosses who were profane, insensitive, totally politically incorrect, and who "appropriated" insignificant items from hotels or the company. We'll visit the mind of a leader who did little but sit in his office (which we considered a good thing). We'll look at another boss who could analyze a highly complex profit-and-loss statement or a balance sheet at a glance, yet who, at times, failed to grasp the simplest financial mechanisms—how things actually worked in practice to *create* the numbers in the real world.

Evaluating these individuals and their idiosyncrasies, I often asked myself if there is, indeed, such a thing as an unflawed leader, one with a true north moral compass, one who consistently demonstrates the ability to communicate clearly and consistently, doesn't get mired in insignificant detail, is steady at the helm in smooth sailing, yet stays calm, rational, and seemingly in control of the situation when an unexpected storm risks capsizing the ship. A leader who motivates, transmits his or her vision with consistency, offers praise for exceptional work, criticism for less-than-perfect accomplishments, and punishment for those who fail to meet expectations repeatedly. Most important, of course, are the results. Did the leader deliver on the stated objective? Did the USMC drill instructor in Parris Island produce combat-ready Marines out of the civilian garbage the recruiting sergeants sent him? Did the high school teacher leave his students with greatly enhanced skills so as to make them successful in their university phase and their chosen careers? In the case of CEOs, did their tenures as heads of their respective companies move the enterprises forward? Was monetary value created for the stakeholders?

For nearly every one of the disparate leaders covered in this book, the final, bottom-line answer is yes. Despite their major personality quirks, some almost unbelievable in scope and quantity, these men (I have never worked for a female leader, I'm sorry to report) were successful.

So, despite, hopefully, an amusing look at the fatuous foibles of some of these illustrious men, not-so-lovingly remembered in those cases where I felt I was the hapless victim, these tales do *not* constitute a "hatchet job" or an attempt at "getting even." The years have caused anger and resentment to dissipate; they are all fundamentally good people. Rather, what I've attempted to do is to show the reader the complexities of successful leaders by exposing both their human weaknesses and, in most cases, their oft-chronicled successes.

I suppose my bottom line is this: most successful leaders are not "average Joes." Like the late Steve Jobs, arguably the most successful business leader of our time, who was often described as harshly uncompromising, mercurial, unfair, impatient, stubborn if not downright unpleasant to deal with, most successful leaders are mentally and emotionally askew. There's a good side, which is great and gets the job done. There's often also a downside that makes them hard to understand or difficult to work for. It's precisely that they are impatient, stubborn, opinionated, unsatisfied, and domineering that makes them successful.

Aspiring leaders can and should take lessons from the cases described herein. They should work on mitigating the bad and emphasizing the good. Leadership is a skill that can be honed. But students of leadership should take heart:

just because you may be abrasive and slightly irrational at times does *not* mean you can't be a great and highly successful leader.

Always make sure that the value you bring to the table consistently and heavily outweighs the negative baggage.

1

GEORGES-ANDRÉ CHEVALLAZ

What's this guy doing as a

high school teacher?

IT WAS a late summer day in 1952 when I, in the company of about twenty other academic misfits from the German part of Switzerland, settled behind my flip-top desk of the École Supérieure de Commerce in Lausanne, the second-largest city in the French-speaking part of Switzerland.

We were there for more or less the same reason: we had mostly all failed to meet the minimum academic or behavioral standards of the high school system in the German-speaking part of Switzerland, for reasons that ranged from what is now fondly referred to as ADD or "attention deficit disorder" (then termed "laziness" or "lack of focus") to insubordinate behavior to outright lack of sufficient intelligence. The first two definitely applied to me.

The common advice the distressed parents had received "up north" was "Look . . . your child is not going to make it in this system. Why not send him/her to the French part of the country? Standards are a little lower, the discipline is a bit more lax, you know . . . a bit more like what you'd expect from the French part of the country. Plus, your child will learn French."

The bell rang, and in strode Georges-André Chevallaz, the man who was to be our principal teacher, provider of homeroom services, instructor in French, business correspondence, literature, French-Swiss history, business law, and pretty much everything except accounting, typing, math, and specialized subjects. Of short stature, he was, nonetheless, an imposing figure. His presence instantly dominated the classroom; he was the epitome of what the U.S. Marine Corps, which I would be joining a few years hence, called "command presence," that indefinable quality that some people possess—an aura of confidence, of knowledge, of unquestionable authority.

His face, with its chiseled features and piercing blue eyes, was straight out of Hollywood central casting for "action hero." He actually bore more than a passing resemblance to Kirk Douglas.

The class fell silent as he stood at attention behind his raised desk. Casting a long, cool gaze upon the assembled Swiss Germans, he finally said, in French, "Welcome, ladies and gentlemen. I look forward to teaching you what you need to be taught. I'm good at it. I demand your attention at all times. I expect respect and will not tolerate talking in class, nor horseplay, nor sloppy work. Assignments will be completed on time and handed in neatly and legibly written. Tests will be both oral and written, announced and unannounced. I set the rules, and you just heard them. And one other thing: out of respect for my position and my considerable education, you will rise when I enter the classroom and be seated when I sit. Any questions? Now is the time to ask. I see there are none, so let's get down to business."

We were all a bit stunned. This was the "kinder, gentler" environment we had escaped to? (Only later did we learn that Mr. Chevallaz was, during school vacations, also serving as one of the youngest field grade officers in the notoriously effective, all-reserve Swiss Army.) Mr. Chevallaz's style was predictably demanding, and he most surely did not tolerate sloppy work.

In language that was reminiscent of the legendary eloquence of Charles de Gaulle, a master practitioner of his tongue, Chevallaz would, from his elevated pedestal, read and critique the compositions that had been handed in the day before. It was usually not a performance for the easily offended or the faint of heart.

His monologues went something like this:

Ah, and now another masterpiece from Monsieur Spaelti (a notorious, often angry underperformer). I see from your congested facial color that you are prepared for another devastating appraisal, and I shall not disappoint. The rambling nature of your turgid diatribe is matched only by the jumbled grammar and syntax of your writing. Were you even dimly aware of the assigned subject, or is this just yet another of your usual polemic, antiestablishment rants? Were it not for my dedication to my students and my unfailing sense of professionalism, I would have cast this so-called "work" into the wastebasket, unread. My verdict: F!

And here is another, this time by the lovely Mademoiselle Streiff. Sadly, it appears that, in your case, considerable physical charm is in sharp contrast to either effort, or intellect, or both. Like some poorly concocted soup, your composition lacks color, substance, and taste. A "thin" piece of work that fails to enrich the reader. D-minus.

And so it went, down the list of every student. Good work was praised, excellent passages were read aloud for all to hear and appreciate. But even favorable appraisals were laced with justified criticisms, suggestions for improvement, alternative use of language. At the end, he never failed to provide a complete picture of how *he* would have approached the subject, and organized the composition for content, readability, and conveyance of the key message.

In addition to the negative, he unfailingly demonstrated the positive. Once the criticism was out of the way, he spent hours working with the chronic underachievers, gradually helping them to attain a level beyond their own expectations. The weak were grateful; the strong were fortified and encouraged. Self-esteem, that quality the American education system seems to want to instill without the rigor of actual performance, was enhanced for all, but with justification.

The young men worshipped him, including me, and even the verbal beatings we took for substandard work, laced with scorn and sarcasm as they were, came to be appreciated and accepted as unpleasant but vital steps in the education process. The females, quite understandably, all had crushes on him. And why not? His towering intellect and his devotion to his profession, coupled with his movie-star looks, were naturally hard to resist. Despite the swooning nature of his female students, he never displayed the slightest inappropriate interest in his obviously smitten charges. He was the consummate, dedicated, honorable, untouchable professional.

So great was he in my eyes that I found myself wondering, "How can a man so talented, of such manifest leadership quality, be relegated to a life of teaching a bunch of Swiss Germans in high school? How and why did a larger career pass him by? How did fame and fortune elude him?" Of course, born in 1915, he was only in his midthirties at the time, and it never occurred to me, viewing him (with the arrogance of youth) as "old," that he still had a full life ahead of him. And what a life it was. He turned to politics, running as a Conservative, and became mayor of Lausanne in 1957, in which capacity he served until 1973.

At the federal level, he was elected a member of the Swiss parliament. In 1973, he was elected to the Federal Council, the seven-person group that collectively forms the executive branch of the Swiss government. He ran the Finance Ministry from 1974 to 1979, the Defense Ministry from 1980 to 1983. And since the seven members of the Federal Council take one-year turns at the largely ceremonial presidency, he was president of Switzerland in 1980.

He wrote several books, including *Switzerland, or the Sleep of the Just* and *The Challenge of Neutrality: Diplomacy and the Defense of Switzerland, 1939–1945*.

From high school teacher to president of his country: it didn't surprise me! Until Chevallaz passed away at eighty-seven in 2002, I stayed in touch with this inspirational person throughout my adult life, once being asked to speak at an event in his honor in Lausanne during my tenure as chairman of Ford of Europe.

Looking at Georges-André Chevallaz through the soft, hazy lens of the kinder, gentler approach to teaching and learning that we espouse today would make us question many aspects of his style. Some tender souls might even call it intellectual bullying; he might well not achieve coveted tenure in an American high school today. But this was the early 1950s, and Europe was recovering from a war. Students were willing to study, and instructors to instruct.

Chevallaz set high standards. I can't speak for his career as a politician because I wasn't there to witness it, but his meteoric rise from a local office to the national presidency has to mean that he impressed with high intelligence, drive, forcefulness, and that he delivered. He was the quintessential old-style leader, the passing of which is so ably lamented in Lee Iacocca's last book, *Where Have All the Leaders Gone?* He conducted no "polls" or "votes" in the class. He did not view his students as equals or pals. He viewed them as raw material, entrusted to him for transformation into young people of more knowledge, skill, character, and focus than before they were entrusted to him. Not everybody passed. The weak were weeded out. But that's part of a leader's role, too. Things that everyone can achieve are rarely considered an achievement. Chevallaz knew that.

In the town where I live there is a middle school whose stated mission is "to imbue every student, regardless of gender, race, or national origin, with a lasting sense of self-esteem, in an environment conducive to learning." In contrast, Chevallaz's mission statement probably would have been, "It is my mission to impart as much knowledge, critical judgment, intellectual curiosity, and character to my students as they can, with hard work, absorb. If I am successful in this task, their achievements will give them a lasting sense of self-esteem."

The impact that Chevallaz had on my life and career went beyond the French language, its rich history and literature. It was his intense dedication, his drive for excellence, and his ability to motivate average students to achieve above-average results that left the most profound mark on me. His ability to use humor as an instrument of praise and to inflict slight embarrassment as a form of punishment shaped my own leadership behavior in the years to come.

2

STAFF SERGEANT DONALD GIUSTO

UNITED STATES MARINE CORPS

Transforming civilian "turds"

into Marines in twelve

not-so-easy weeks.

AFTER GRADUATING from the High School of Commerce in Lausanne in 1954, at the ripe age of twenty-two (I was a slow learner and Swiss school is thirteen and a half years), I honored a commitment made to my father in exchange for his generous funding of one last (ultimately successful) effort at education: I got on a plane to New York, stayed with friends of my parents, and went to the local USMC recruiting station.

A kindly sergeant asked me what specialty I would like the corps to bestow upon me. With alacrity (having consumed every Marine aviation epic, including *Flying Leathernecks,* multiple times), I replied, "I want to be a Marine fighter pilot."

"Well, that's great, son. Do you have a college degree? No? Well, then you can't go directly into the aviation program, but see, I can enlist you for two years, and once you're in, you can apply for flight training, and I'm most sure you'll get it." He neglected to tell me that the chance of getting into the Marine aviator program that way is, oh, about one in a thousand, but it didn't matter: I signed up!

Ten days later, I was on a train to Yemassee, South Carolina, with a motley band of greasy-haired kids from the east side of New York, a few youthful criminals from the Rhode Island State Penitentiary who received shortened sentences in exchange for service in the Marines, as well as a few bright-eyed kids who looked reasonably tidy. All were full of confidence. The Puerto Ricans, especially, flashed knives and said they definitely were not going to take crap from any drill instructor!

The tone changed quickly when all of us, clutching our meager belongings, were forcibly dragged from the rail cars by bellowing Marines who were visibly beside themselves with anger, even though we had done nothing wrong. Confused, tired, disoriented, we assembled on the now-famous yellow footprints and were marched off by shrill-screaming NCOs, rightfully disgusted by the long-haired, ill-dressed group of new "turds" that the recruiting sergeants had dumped on them. Hours later, showered, bereft of all our civilian goods (the Puerto Ricans' knives were seized and summarily snapped in half), heads shaved totally bare, our arms groaning under the load of USMC-issued uniforms, athletic gear, shoes, boots, etc., we were herded to the World War II–vintage wooden barracks, which would be our "home," so to speak, for the next twelve weeks.

It was there that our temporary hosts handed us over to the man who would, in his own words, be our mother, father, priest, judge, Jesus Christ, Holy Ghost, God and, if warranted, executioner. He was SSgt Donald Giusto, senior drill instructor (DI). We were now Platoon 258-54, and we belonged to him.

About five foot ten, he was massively built but devoid of fat. Broad shoulders, powerful chest, narrow hips, sturdy neck—his starched, pressed, field-green utility uniform fit him as if it had been tailored on Savile Row. His face showed early evidence of the jowls that would probably emerge later in life. Not given to wearing sunglasses (he liked eye contact), his eyes were narrowed in a near-permanent squint. He was visibly disappointed with the latest pile of human garbage that "the idiot recruiters, who'd enlist their moms if necessary to make the quota" had sent him this time.

Spotting an Asian-looking recruit, Giusto proceeded to express his hatred for the race: the Chinese had shot him in Korea. But, ever fair in his views, he quickly added that he strongly disliked blacks, Jews, Hispanics, and whites, *unless* they were Marines. And we clearly were not, nor would we probably ever be. We were much too sorry a collection this time.

SSgt Giusto had learned from the Koreans that while squatting on one's haunches is totally comfortable for most Asians (it's a common position in their cultures, especially in more rural areas), it's hugely uncomfortable for Westerners and acutely painful for more than a few minutes. Thus, when not standing at attention, we squatted while our drill instructor imparted wisdom. Those in pain were tempted to sit or kneel, which was instantly punished. Worse, since we clearly weren't fit to march, we were herded around the squad bay walking in the squatted position. It was called "duck walking," and what a sight it was: odd-uniformed (loose, unpressed green utilities), bald young men of every race, waddling painfully, looking for all the world like a herd of ducks. "Faster, you turds! We haven't got all day!" So the pace picked up. The pain in our hip and ankle joints as well as our back muscles was excruciating.

One large Hispanic recruit had soon had enough and dared to challenge SSgt Giusto's authority, lunging for him while shouting obscenities. Faster than the blink of an eye, it seemed, the Hispanic youth was hit, kicked, kneed, rabbit-punched, and neatly folded on the floor, holding various portions of his anatomy and moaning softly. "Anybody else wanna try me on?" shouted Giusto. "We may as well get it out of the way, and I'm just getting warmed up! You over there . . . you look tough, come on, come on!" There were no takers. We were all awestruck. Giusto then solicitously bent over the felled recruit, made sure there was no permanent damage, and placed him back into the duck walk position.

As the days and weeks passed, we learned more and more about the corps and about ourselves. Clearly, we learned to march properly (especially during "close-order drill," where platoons would compete against one another, and drill instructors hated to lose to colleagues) and perform the "manual of arms," the carefully mass-choreographed manipulation of the eight-pound M-1 rifle.

But we also learned that we could stand at attention in front of our bunks, not moving a muscle, for hours. We learned that bodily functions could be timed: endless standing at attention would be relieved by the rare "five-minute head call," which sent eighty recruits to a limited number of urinals and back to attention in the allotted time, or else.

Occasionally, some hapless recruit would, while at attention, shout, "Sir! Private Walker requests permission to speak to the drill instructor. Sir!"

"Speak up, turd!"

"Sir, Private Walker needs to go to the head awful bad!"

SSgt Giusto would glance at his watch and say, "You're in trouble, turd. The next head call isn't scheduled until an hour from now. But you know what they say: shame is better than pain! Ya got that?"

"Yes, sir."

About ten minutes later, the rigidly standing Private Walker started to tremble, and a dark stain of urine spread from his groin down his trousers, over his boots, and into a widening puddle on the scrubbed wooden floor. This provoked a harsh lecture on the evils of poor hygiene, drinking too much water, not having control and discipline over one's body, and an impromptu one-man floor mop-up. Unscheduled urination soon stopped.

Hygiene loomed large in SSgt Giusto's list of virtues. The recruits cleaned all urinals and toilet bowls twice daily. But since the purpose was to become accustomed to the scarcity prevalent in combat conditions, we had no cleaning tools. No brushes, no rags, no scouring powder. "Use your precious little hands, you stupid turds!" was the answer to the problem of how to clean all those bowls with none of the usual tools. We were given buckets of fine Parris Island sand, told to scoop a handful, and then rub it into every nook and cranny of every bowl and urinal, applying a good flush at the end, which also served to rinse our hands off. At our house, at home, the maids cleaned the toilets: now I was using my bare hands, and it was with mixed feelings that I approached the task. I felt I couldn't do it but was deathly afraid not to try, so I did it. Weirdly, after the first few urinals, it became easy: my hands didn't burn or develop lesions. It was sand, water, and porcelain, no big deal. It became routine.

SSgt Giusto's lesson: one can't let learned reactions of revulsion and disgust stand in the way of doing what needs to be done. In combat, a badly wounded buddy might be a bloody mess, too awful even to contemplate. But the duty is to reach out, reach in, get covered in his blood, and do what needs to be done to save his life. My days of bare-handed toilet cleaning have helped me often in later life. I can deal with truly disgusting situations where others walk away.

We also learned how to deal with extreme fatigue and keep going. One day, we were marched to the PX and told to buy one glass bottle of Clorox each. We obediently marched back to the squad bay and turned over an arsenal of eighty Clorox bottles to SSgt Giusto.

Then, while we stood at attention in front of our bunks, SSgt Giusto's two assistant drill instructors, Sgt Davis and Corporal Gagnepain, brought in four buckets of fine sand, which they proceeded to strew over the floor, bunks, and locker boxes. This task completed, SSgt Giusto started at one end of the squad bay, brandished a bottle of Clorox in each hand, and smashed them together, sending quarts of undiluted Clorox and shards of glass raining to the floor. His two assistants trailed him, always handing him two more bottles as he slowly worked his way down the squad bay. Needless to say, although afraid to move our eyes, we nevertheless witnessed these bizarre proceedings with trepidation: we knew *who* was going to clean it up, but how?

Easy! On our hands and knees, with dustpans and our

own little individual scrub brushes. We found the big shards of glass; the small ones found us: every recruit had red-stained trousers from countless small cuts on his knees. Hands were bloody, too, and sore from the undiluted Clorox which, incidentally, gave off toxic odors. The good news: the cuts were disinfected by the Clorox as fast as they occurred. It was grueling, but in two hours, the floor was dry and free of sand, glass, and Clorox.

SSgt Giusto surveyed the scene with what we were sure was approval. He shouted, "Okay, everybody, FALL OUT!" Eighty recruits shot through the doorway and assembled in the now-darkness on the tarmac. Now what? We were hardly prepared for the scene we witnessed once we went back inside the squad bay: more buckets of sand were dispersed, and the remaining Clorox bottles were meeting their now-familiar fate! Only this time, all forty double bunks were overthrown, the bedding joining the sandy, Clorox-infused mess. The recruits were demoralized beyond reasonable description: the more astute could understand the reason, arcane as it might be, for the first round of destruction and defilement. And we had done our duty and bled and cleaned it up. But now, all this *again* . . . it made no sense. It was late, we were wet with Clorox, blood-soaked, red-eyed, dog-tired. There was a sense of disbelief. . . . They can't have done it again! Well, they *had* done it again, and as tired and worn-out as we were, we cleaned it all up again, completing the task by about 2:00 A.M.

The lesson, in this case, was that things don't go as planned; they can go horribly wrong. An enemy force can be cleared from a position at great cost in time, ammunition, even lives, only to have a superior force retake the position late in the day. The Marines, beaten, bloodied, counting their losses, surely wouldn't attack again, this late in the day. News flash: if told to do so, they would, and would tell themselves, "No worse than cleaning up the damn squad bay twice." Learning to continue to function in the face of failure, betrayal, acute disappointment, all the while physically and mentally tired, perhaps without food, is what the Marine Corps expects from its members. What it demonstrated to me is that we are all capable, when the chips are down, of doing far more than we think we can. SSgt Giusto unlocked the hidden reservoirs of capability in all of us.

Humiliation, individual or collective, was very much in the DI's bag of tricks.

It was all part of the Marine Corps' deliberate destruction of unwanted civilian values, loyalties to past things, such as high schools, civilian friends, even relatives and parents. With regard to the latter, SSgt Giusto expressed mostly disdain, claiming that "Momma" had obviously done a rotten job raising "Junior," had committed serious errors of omission which now, sadly, were making his job so much more difficult. The mailing of cookies to recruits could not be prevented but was seen as a serious threat to recruits' health as well as an unwanted reminder of the comfort of a mother's love and baking skill. Clearly, these were elements unwanted in a future warrior. To limit the damage, SSgt Giusto, during mail call, would ask the recruit's permission to open the package. He then slashed it open with his Ka-Bar (a special USMC combat knife), and upon spying the carefully arranged brownies, would distribute most to him-self and his two assistant drill instructors. The legitimate recipient was then made to eat the remainder on the spot, while standing at attention. Packages of food soon dried up in no longer than the time necessary for postcards to reach various mothers.

A future problem, also involving mothers, was the much-dreaded "Mothers' Visiting Day," viewed by SSgt Giusto as a further decline in Marine standards of tough-ness, a coddling of recruits who needed the opposite, and, worst of all, a wasted training day. But regulations required that he inform us of our right to have our mothers come visit. (In my case, it was moot; my mother would not have dreamed of flying from Switzerland for the event.)

In relaying the required message, SSgt Giusto took care to point out, in no uncertain and rather graphic de-tail, that we would, of course, be confined to the squad bay after our (early) "evening chores." The mothers, however, would still be around and would be invited to the NCO (noncommissioned officers) club by him. They would be encouraged to drink, and when sufficiently drunk, the at-tractive ones would fall victim to the good SSgt's sexual whims. Miraculously, Mothers' Visiting Day came and went. Not a single mother showed up. It was just another train-ing day.

The techniques of sleep deprivation, physical discom-fort, humiliation, scorn for all civilian values and non-Marine life in general, all wrapped in high levels of stress, had been honed and perfected by the corps for centuries. All DIs learned the drill in DI school, but some took to it with more enthusiasm than others. SSgt Giusto was a master practitioner!

This phase, lasting roughly half of the twelve-week period, was followed as it is today, by a reprogramming of the now-purified, zero-based brains of the recruits.

The remaining time would be spent not in the deconstruction of the civilian but in the creation of a Marine, with the requisite weapons skills, stamina, knowledge of first aid, familiarity with small unit tactics, ever greater perfection in close-order drill and the manual of arms. SSgt Giusto switched from the role of punitive slave driver to one of professional teacher and coach, spending hours on Marine history, traditions, chain of command, the Uniform Code of Military Justice, the love of one's fellow Marines, and, above all, the guiding principles of duty, honor, and commitment.

At some point in this process, I was taken out of training for one day and flown to Charleston Naval Hospital to assess my physical and mental suitability for Marine Aviation. Obviously, the intelligence test we had all taken on arrival had produced the result so wrongfully promised by the New York recruiting sergeant. I was ultimately selected, went to flight training, became a commissioned officer, and flew Marine fighter and attack jets until 1965. My orders to Pensacola, however, were not to come until well after my completion of boot camp. Upon my return from Charleston, SSgt Giusto called me to his tiny office and asked me how it had gone. When I told him I thought I had done well and was hoping for selection, he said, "Well, that would be a goddamn shame! You, a friggin' officer, and a zoomie at that! I was hoping that someday you'd become a really good infantry sergeant, like me!"

It was the highest (and only) compliment I was ever to receive from SSgt Don Giusto. Abusive, profane, vulgar, cruel with a purpose, a master of sarcasm (often hilarious, but laughter was severely punished) and mental and physical intimidation, he would not pass muster in today's caring, solicitous, love-and-tolerance-infested civilian world. It would not even fit well in today's somewhat sanitized Marine Corps.

And yet, nobody was permanently scarred except for the 18–20 percent of the platoon that dropped out for "psychological" reasons; the attrition, while painful, was exactly what the corps wanted. The psychologically tender, vulnerable souls would not have been reliable Marines in actual combat. Curiously, the attrition rate in boot camp remains about the same today. All the rest of us became fine Marines; many stayed in the corps and enjoyed a fine military career. All, including me, found a permanent, reliable set of moral rules which, while secular, transcend those offered by various religions.

In the words of the late president Ronald Reagan, "Many people go through life wondering if they have made a difference. Marines do not have that problem."

SSgt Giusto achieved that result in the many platoons he transformed from civilian "turds" into combat-capable Marines.

If some of his methods were beyond those officially sanctioned by the Marine Corps at the time, I forgive him: he was one of the great leaders in my life. Other drill instructors may have used the same methods and achieved the same results. And no Marine, regardless of age, ever forgets his drill instructor.

SSgt Donald M. Giusto was special: he was *my* drill instructor. And what can a Marine drill instructor with only a high school diploma possibly contribute to a long and successful career in large corporations? My flippant reply would be "More than any MBA degree!" But, to be specific, he taught the values of duty, honor, and commitment, of perseverance under hardship, of mental and physical pain as a necessary milestone in the achievement of a goal. He taught me that, in successful leadership, it isn't just education and intellect that matter. It's the power of will, focus, self-sacrifice, and dedication to a higher goal that can not only make scared teenagers perform brilliantly in combat but also drive often-confused corporate employees, frequently confronted with an overwhelming array of conflicting objectives, toward success.

3

ROBERT "BOB" WACHTLER

DIRECTOR OF FORWARD PLANNING
GM OVERSEAS OPERATIONS
1960–1965

Does he know any words

besides four-letter ones?

AFTER FIVE years' active duty in the Marine Corps, I attended UC Berkeley in what is now called the Haas School of Business, made a living as a Marine Reserve aviator and a vacuum cleaner salesman, and quite enjoyed the academic world. I graduated in 1962, with highest honors, and planned to join the Ford Motor Company after a one-year academic assignment in Europe.

My father, the banker, considered this a poor choice. "What happened with General Motors? Didn't they want you?" "That wasn't it," I explained. "GM doesn't interview on the West Coast. They've found that Californians hate Detroit and soon go back." Dad considered this to be a thin excuse, and since he knew Fred Donner, at that time CEO of GM, from his banking days in New York, he initiated a contact, which triggered a series of interviews that, in turn, resulted in my being hired as a senior analyst in the Forward Planning Department of General Motors Overseas Operations.

My starting salary was to be $8,000—derisory in today's anemic dollars, but this was in 1963, when the average middle-class home cost $35,000, hamburgers were 15 cents, gasoline was around 30 cents a gallon, and the average new car cost $2,500. So, multiply by ten and you've got a reasonable starting salary. I was thrilled.

Somehow, somebody had neglected to inform Mr. Bob
Wachtler that I had been hired into his small, presumably
elite team, and this was to make for a stormy welcome. On
my first day, I reported to him. I was immaculately dressed
and ready to impress. I knocked on the open door, and a
loud, deep voice shouted, "Come on in, goddammit! Who
the hell told you to knock?" He was a big man. In his early
sixties, he had the beefy, congested appearance of a former
wrestler or pro football linebacker who had let himself get
out of shape. His hair was close-cropped white, the prominent nose was flanked by pronounced cheekbones which,
in turn, formed a visual counterpoint to jowls lower down
on his massive face. When he rose, it was clear that his substantial frame was anything but agile. His head moved
hardly at all on what passed for a neck—it was more a
slightly thinner extension of the torso, blending smoothly
into his enormous head.

As I walked toward him, he extended a massive hand,
easily the size of a medium-weight ham. It grasped mine,
painfully. "Sit down!" he grumped, as he plopped himself
down in his leather chair and fixed a steely gaze on me
from behind the paper-festooned desk. His stare was cold,
unwelcoming, with nary a twinkle that might have hinted at
a sense of humor buried somewhere. "Look," he began, "I
didn't hire you . . . don't need you . . . wasn't asked." (He
spoke in staccato, high-volume bursts, with little change in
tone or inflection.) "But my boss, Phil Copelin, says I gotta
take you, so I will!"

With that, he shuffled through some papers, retrieved
my file, and began to read my resumé, rife with business

school academic-speak, which I had naïvely assumed would have a killer impact on any future employer. "Look!" (It was his favorite opener.) "I've read your fancy friggin' resumé about six times, and I still don't understand what any of those long words mean. I guess they taught you a lot of new-fangled ultramodern crap at Berkeley. Well, it ain't gonna do you no good in *my* department, because when it comes to the way we do business we're in the goddamn Stone Age, and the best advice I can give you if you want to last more than a week is to forget your education and just Stone Age it along with the rest of us. Savvy?"

I was somewhat stunned: here was the international planning function of the world's foremost industrial conglomerate, and it was being led by a person of profoundly anti-intellectual attitude who looked and dressed as if he had just completed a hard day of lifting and replacing cast-iron manhole covers for the New York Department of Sanitation. Of what use now was the time I spent mastering game theory, multiplayer probabilistic outcomes, quadratic programming, dynamic programming, projective surveying techniques, and all the other mostly math-based quantitative techniques for which UC Berkeley at the time was famous?

"Go see Kris Kristoff. You'll report to him. I hope to Christ he's got something for you to do that you won't screw up." This ended my first encounter with my very first non-academic, nonmilitary leader.

My expectations for Forward Planning's output and value to the company were low, but in retrospect, Bob Wachtler's somewhat brutal introduction displayed considerable courage and honesty: he readily confessed his limited education and his failure to understand the pseudointellectual business-school-speak of my overblown resumé. He acknowledged his resentment over my hiring without his involvement, and he artfully reset my expectations, told me what the culture was like, and provided me with the framework in which I was to operate. It was a classic example of honest, no-holds-barred leadership communication. No pretense, no sugarcoating, no "how does this make me look?" Just the plain, hard facts.

Over the years—and often at the receiving end of favorable, seemingly positive, platitude-rich appraisals by my bosses, during which I sensed an undertone of "I'm not quite satisfied"—I often longed for the equivalent of that simple, direct Wachtler speech, which left no room for ambiguity. Too many leaders are timid and fearful in their downward communication, worried that they might somehow cause pain, anger, discouragement, or resignation. Far better to sugarcoat the message, get it out of the way, and be able to report "I counseled him on his behavior."

Wachtler was not a master of formal written communication. Tasked with drafting a letter to some senior individual within the company, I would enter his office, paper in hand, knowing that it conveyed the message and was ready to be typed and sent. Wachtler would take it from me and stare at it intently for minutes, slightly moving his lips, audibly reading passages out loud again and again. "I don't know," he'd say. "It's not . . . bad . . . it's just . . . maybe too polite . . . maybe I want the SOB to know we're pissed off . . . just don't be too obvious. Here, see what you can do."

The second, third, and fourth efforts still failed to hit the "Aha!" spot. Bob Wachtler would call in every direct report, plus his faithful secretary and me. He would go to great lengths explaining the purpose of the letter and why the current proposals didn't quite hit the mark, and would then group-wordsmith the document, with all six or eight meeting participants suggesting alternative letter structure, opening, flow, vocabulary, tone, and syntax. It was a laborious process, often consuming half an hour per paragraph. Once completed, Bob Wachtler would read the collective product out loud only to notice that our disjointed effort had produced redundancies. Growing angry, he would pound the conference table in frustration, hurling a barrage of four-letter filth at no one in particular. His tirades always ended with him patting the hand of his patient secretary, sitting on his immediate right to "take the letter," and saying in a low, fatherly voice, "I'm terribly sorry you had to hear all that, my dear!" She would just nod politely. She'd heard the same thing hundreds of times, and she'd achieved a level of tolerance bordering on complete immunity.

Bob Wachtler was not without a sense of humor, however racist, sexist, homophobic, and species-ist it may have been. Let's remember that we're talking about a white, predominantly German-origin male in his early sixties, and the year was 1963. Different standards were in effect.

One day, we were discussing the future assembly of pickup trucks in a Latin American country. Since all countries with automotive ambitions mandated a rising percentage of locally produced components, it was a constant battle to find indigenous producers who could meet the cost and quality targets. Wachtler liked the idea of sourcing major rear axle components, like the cast-iron differential housing and the lateral axle tubes, to local suppliers and then assembling the axles in the GM plant.

The truck folks and the quality group (neither of which reported to Wachtler) were worried that local casting and forming capability was too immature. They favored sourcing some other components locally and shipping the rear axles fully assembled, ready to bolt into the chassis. Bob became frustrated. He fixed his antagonists with an icy stare, slapped his hand down so hard that the coffee cups bounced, and intoned, "Look . . . I spent years and years in those goddamn countries, and I wanna tell you sumpin'. Ya can't ship built-up axles to South America because all the goddamn dagos in the ports will suck all the friggin' grease out of them." ("Oh, I'm sorry you had to hear that, my dear!")

The conference room was stunned for a few seconds, but I, ever a fan of political incorrectness, burst out laughing. Once I did so, Bob Wachtler began to laugh until, seconds later, the big hand slammed the table again. "Look, goddammit, we've got entirely too much levity here, and it's gotta stop. We got serious work to do!" I don't remember the outcome of the axle-sourcing discussion. The memorable highlight was Bob Wachtler's colorful comment.

On another occasion, he had his fun with a subordinate named Norm Heaney. Norm was, in many ways, the polar opposite of Bob Wachtler. Slight of build, bespectacled, soft-spoken, meticulous in dress and grooming (his tailoring suggested J. Press or Brooks Brothers, with more than a passing nod to a tweedy, Ivy League professional look), and erudite, Heaney spoke in well-structured, complete sentences and eschewed vulgarity and profanity. This was in sharp contrast to Wachtler's staccato, grunted salvos, followed by heavy pauses, with an F-word or two linking the content at either end. It would be fair to say that these two were not comfortable in each other's presence.

They did share one thing, though. They both wore hearing aids, which in those days featured an earpiece the size of a quarter, with wires running to a pretty massive, pink, kidney-shaped plastic housing hooked to the top of the ear. From its station behind the ear, more wires ran to a device the size of two cigarette packs, on top of which sat the volume control knob. This "radio" was usually worn in the breast pocket of a shirt or jacket.

One day, it seems, Heaney was in Bob Wachtler's office explaining something in his usual, painfully didactic manner. "Speak up, can't you?" shouted Bob. "I can't hear a word you're mumbling." Norm Heaney suggested that maybe Bob should turn up his hearing aid. Wachtler, irritated, insisted there was nothing wrong with his hearing aid, and somewhat indelicately asked Heaney to get out and submit it all in writing.

A few days later, Wachtler called a large meeting. We were all grouped around his long conference table, but Norm Heaney was missing. Wachtler explained that this was to be no ordinary meeting. Indeed, its purpose would be to teach Norm Heaney "a little humility." "The guy thinks he knows hearing aids. I'm gonna show him he doesn't have a clue, so here's what we're gonna do. I'll start out in a normal voice, but over time, I'll speak more and more softly. Act normal, but always answer me no louder than I'm talking, savvy? At the end, we'll just move our lips, with no goddamn sound at all. Do you guys think you can do that? Good!" (To his secretary, in a kind, fatherly tone, "Go call Norm Heaney in, my dear.")

In came Norm and took his seat. Bob Wachtler introduced the bogus subject, and soon began to lower his voice. Norm reached into his jacket, and surreptitiously turned his volume up. We all played our parts as the exchanges became ever less audible. And time after time, Norm reached for his breast pocket and twisted the knob to "louder." Finally, when we were all just moving our lips, Norm made his last available adjustment: the volume was at max!

When Wachtler saw that the desperate Heaney had made the last, fatal knob twist, he banged his fist on the conference table with a resounding, cup-rattling boom, and simultaneously shouted, " . . . AND SO, HERE'S WHAT WE'RE GONNA DO!!" To say that poor Norm had to be scraped off the ceiling would obviously be a gross exaggeration. But that phrase does conjure up the proper imagery of what actually transpired. The bewildered Norm Heaney desperately grappled with the volume control and was so embarrassed that he was near tears. Bob Wachtler's thigh-slapping guffaws didn't help, especially as none of us could contain our mirth over this successful prank against an individual with an "auditory challenge." Even in those days of bigotry, racism, cripple jokes, and more, the only thing that made it even marginally acceptable was that Wachtler's hearing was worse than Heaney's.

So, the gentle reader may ask, of what use was such a leader, with his lack of education, polish, sophistication, and couth?

Simple. In an environment of rampant interdepartmental rivalry and in a building crammed full of GM's ponderous staffs, projects moved at a snail's pace. One step forward could take weeks, only to be upset by some other staff jamming an analytical stick into the spokes of advancement, resulting in a return to square one. Bob Wachtler was the mighty bulldozer of progress.

Many times, I would hear him shout to his secretary, "My dear, get me that guy over in Finance who sent that stupid goddamn memo!" What followed usually went something like this: "Look. Wachtler here. I read your stupid memo, and it's clear to me that you don't get it. I can't waste my time explaining it all again, so just rewrite the f—ing thing, and this time, recommend approval. Savvy? And I want it on my desk before you go home, whenever the hell that is." Click!

Wachtler used his subordinates for his creative and intellectual firepower. He was demanding and wasn't happy until we had delivered the tools that would permit him to win. Then he used the arsenal provided with devastating effect, arguing, cajoling, threatening up and down the line, battling for GM's business expansion in the far-flung international markets, laying the foundation for today, when almost 70 percent of GM's volume is outside the United States. This was hard slogging in a corporate environment that was heavily U.S.-centric in its thinking and priorities, and which considered an assignment to "overseas" as punitive, or the last refuge for executives who couldn't cut the mustard in one of the domestic divisions.

Bob Wachtler, the aging, battle-scarred survivor of countless internecine battles, the pit bull in a roomful of toy poodles, profane, unsophisticated intimidator that he was, got the job done.

GM and I owe him a huge debt.

4

RALPH MASON

CHAIRMAN OF THE MANAGEMENT BOARD
ADAM OPEL AG
1966–1970

The trouble with being a

teetotaler is waking up at

8:00 A.M. and realizing that

that's the best you're gonna

feel all day.

RALPH MASON was novel in many ways. He was perhaps the first real counter to the popularly held corporate belief that General Motors Overseas Operations was being run much like an exclusive club, with little desire for technical or human input from the GM mother ship. It's true that many GMOO executives were graduates of Dartmouth, that they followed a time-honored career path starting with small sales operations or assembly plants, moving to larger responsibility and operations, ultimately to land as CEO of one of GMOO's "big three": Opel, Holden, or Vauxhall. It's also true that breeding and command of the social graces played a large part in their career progression. The real work at the various stations of their careers was, of course, performed by an increasingly capable cadre of indigenous executives, none of whom could ever aspire to top leadership positions in that era.

One senior GM domestic executive wanted to have dinner with me after two days of business meetings with Ralph Mason's predecessor. "I don't get it," he said. "I spent two days with the guy, and all he wants to talk about is which restaurant we're gonna go to, how it's in such-and-such old castle, and then he goes on and on about the goddamn wines! Doesn't anybody ever talk about cars and the business?" As diplomatically as I could, I let on that many of the younger people shared his frustration.

It was partly because of this frustration with the "GMOO gang" that GM Corporate decided to try something new: instead of a polished, ticked-all-the-boxes GMOO veteran taking over Opel (at that time GM's second-largest vehicle entity behind Chevrolet), let's try some hard-hitting, two-fisted "domestic" guy we all like!

So Ralph Mason, accompanied by his wife, Rina, left his job as head of Chevrolet manufacturing and found himself living in a palatial home provided to the CEO of Adam Opel AG in Rüsselsheim, Germany. Ralph spoke not a word of German or any other language for that matter (most of the career GMOO varsity team spoke at least one). Given the U.S.-centricity of GM at that time, it's doubtful that he knew much, if anything, about Opel before getting the job.

Still, this did not faze him. An imposing figure at six foot three and roughly 250 pounds, his large, porpoise-shaped body was crowned by a long, long face, its oval appearance magnified by a high forehead above which a wispy reddish comb-over fought in vain to hide the massive, somewhat pointy head. Adding to the impression of "longest face ever" was the fact that Ralph, then in his early sixties, had no discernible chin. From his lower lip, a smooth curve of ruddy fat arced gracefully down to his shirt collar. Not "fat" by contemporary American standards, he was "rotund," "heavily built," or "potbellied."

Ralph was from Georgia and spoke with a pronounced "Suthin'" accent, which caused major comprehension problems for the German personnel, accustomed as they were to the clearly and impeccably enunciated English of the GMOO-Dartmouth clique. After a few initial meetings with Ralph Mason, we were unsure exactly why he had been sent to us. Nothing in his professional career would seem to have qualified him; he'd never had product development responsibility, had never been exposed to sales or marketing, and had never run an integrated, multifunctional organization. He had come up through the manufacturing ranks, and that was it. This fact, coupled with his utter cluelessness about Europe in general and Germany in particular, had us all shaking our heads. We knew domestic GM was going to inject some new blood into the inbred GMOO culture, but why the "gen'mun fum Georgia," as he liked to refer to himself? The answer soon became apparent: Ralph, aided and abetted by the lovely (if slightly leathery) Rina, was a major alcoholic.

This became obvious at the first dinner meeting with major German Opel dealers, during which Ralph proceeded to drink himself into a state of unconsciousness. Two of the taller district managers from my sales staff had to drag him to the hotel elevator, his expensive wingtip shoes, toes down, scraping along the flagstone floor. Rina, barely ambulatory herself, accompanied the trio, repeatedly instructing the two district managers to "Jes' get 'im to the room and on a bed."

This answered a question we all had: why did he rarely arrive at the office before 10:00, and why did he always glance nervously at his watch after about 4:00 P.M., suddenly announcing, "Gotta go, gents! Ah got an impohtant meetin' downtown"? The "impohtant meetin' " turned out to be with Rina at a swanky Frankfurt bar named New Jimmy's. Here, night after night, Ralph and Rina would proceed to get hopelessly plastered, then be driven home and aided inside by his driver and security personnel.

Suddenly, we understood the logic of this unusual career move: Ralph's drinking had become an embarrassment to Chevrolet, and in a then time-honored GM tradition, Ralph was "recycled" into GMOO. ("Not good enough for the big time here in the United States, but better than anyone they have in GMOO" went the thinking.)

Ralph was not a benevolent drunk. Cheerful and humorous when sober, he'd typically start meetings with jokes, often off-color or racist ones. (GMOO was lily-white in those days, as was most of GM.) But when drunk, usually shortly before descending into a lifeless 250-pound lump of carefully tailored pickled flesh, he could turn nasty, which I discovered one night at a party. While sober, he professed great admiration for my person and my job performance. After his first half dozen highballs, he took me aside and said, "You're a goddamn fahn young man, and Ah'm gonna see that you move fast."

This was repeated, verbatim, as the alcoholic stupor gradually settled in. When I decided it was time to leave the party and go to my room, politeness demanded that I say good night.

Ralph, at this point, sat alone at a table, jacket off, tie loosened, elbows on the table, glass in hand. Slowly, his massive face showed he was aware of my presence. "Good night, Ralph. Thanks for the conversation," I said. He slowly sat upright, locked my eyes in a gaze that was somehow both steely and watery, and said, "Get off mah suedes, you arrogant piece of shit."

Another time, not quite as drunk, he proceeded to tell me of his favorable view of an upcoming Opel Commodore sports luxury station wagon to be called the Voyage, but which, this being Europe, was pronounced to rhyme with "garage" (voy-ahge).

"We're gonna do the Vaahge."

"Sorry, Ralph . . . how's that?"

"Vaahge!"

"I still don't understand. Could you repeat that?"

"Vaahge! Vaahge! VAAHGE!! You're supposed to speak French, you dumb fuck!"

Thus ended yet another evening with me wondering about my future. But, happily, eight to nine hours of booze-induced unconsciousness appeared to erase these conversations from his mind.

Ralph was cheerful about his drinking. "Ah love to drink, and so does Rina. Sometimes, we ask ourselves if maybe we should stop. But you know the trouble with bein' a teetotaler? You wake up at eight o'clock in the morning, knowing that's as good as you're gonna feel all day!" He would then let loose with loud, openmouthed guffaws, until joke time was over and he would adopt a serious mien and say, "Okay, let's get on with this here meetin'."

The Masons' regular patronage of New Jimmy's ended badly, however. It seems that one fine evening, both Ralph and Rina were beyond the blissful stage when Rina suddenly discovered her purse was gone. Flailing around, she complained loudly that some SOB had stolen her purse, which had been "right here, next to me." Ralph insisted the police be called, and the manager was forced to tell the other guests that "nobody leave this place" until the cops checked everyone out.

The Frankfurt police arrived in force and proceeded to search the joint. The purse was found, intact, on a hook behind the ladies' room stall door that Rina had visited perhaps thirty minutes before the "theft" was discovered. Neither the manager nor the police nor the other patrons were amused, and shortly thereafter, Ralph received a formal letter from New Jimmy's that his business was no longer desired. A sad outcome for what had started as a rollicking good evening!

Ralph gave little in the way of clear direction in meetings, preferring to rely on his highly competent direct reports. By some strange happenstance, Opel at the time had some of GM's finest up-and-comers in Design, Engineering, Finance, and Manufacturing. With Ralph's lack of sales and marketing experience, I pretty much ran my area with little interference or, indeed, interest on his part.

My office was just down the hall from his, and this resulted in frequent calls on the intercom saying, "Bob, Ah got Harlow Gage on the line. He wants to know how things are goin'. Come on down to mah office." (Gage was the regional director for Opel, Vauxhall, and Holden. Amazingly, although every car division general manager in the United States was a vice president at the time, Harlow, who was in charge of three, *reported to* a vice president. Another sign of the low esteem in which GMOO was held.)

With no speakerphone, Ralph would scribble notes to me like "wants sales numbers, share this month." I would scribble the answers while Ralph stalled for time. "Lemme see, Harlow, Ah got it raaht here. Ah pretty much know it, but Ah'd rather give it to you accurately," meanwhile waving me on to greater speed with his free hand. "Okay, Harlow, Ah got it, and it's lookin' good, like I said." And then he would artfully expound on the information provided. "Ah am on top of it, Harlow, trust me. Ah am pushin' Bob and the boys, believe me," etc. The call usually lasted about thirty action-packed minutes, and, given the six-hour time difference between New York and Rüsselsheim, was usually followed by Ralph's departure for a "big meetin' down in Frankfurt."

Obviously, Ralph Mason was more than a semi-washed-up high-level alcoholic. There was a core of toughness and courage about him that sometimes appeared when least expected. Like all good leaders, once locked in on logic and the right decision, he pursued what he wanted. One such instance involved the sourcing of the body stamping, body-in-white (the unpainted steel shell), paint, trim, and final assembly of the Opel GT, a two-passenger sports coupe looking vaguely like a smaller version of a period Corvette. It could not be built in any of the busy Opel plants, so "contract build" by an outside company was the only option.

The German establishment, the cadre of indigenous executives in engineering, manufacturing, and purchasing, all defaulted to Karmann, a well-regarded contract manufacturer remembered best for the remarkable VW Karmann Ghia coupe of the 1960s. There was no doubt that Karmann possessed the capability of executing the manufacturing portion of the Opel GT program with quality, on time, and within budget, but the latter was the problem. Through a contact I had established, Opel had also received a well-structured, abundantly documented bid from the French metal stamper, coach builder, and contract assembler Brissonneau et Lotz. Highly regarded in France, B & L had its plants running at near capacity producing vehicles for French manufacturers, usually low-to-medium-volume body styles that the companies could not accommodate in their own plants. Brissonneau's quality was highly regarded, and our "due diligence" conversations with leading French auto executives confirmed that it would make a reliable, high-performance partner. To top it off, both the investment estimate as well as the per-unit manufacturing charge were as much as 40 percent below those of Karmann.

One would think, in a rational world, this would be an easy decision, but as the reader knows, corporations do not always hew to the rational. This was the late 1960s, and the Germans at Opel still harbored many of the stereotypical beliefs about the French: the food and wine are good, they are bon vivants, but they don't work hard and have trouble making good products, with inferior French airplanes, tanks, and infantry weapons in World War II being cited as "proof."

Two principal factions soon evolved. The resident American executives, looking at the two proposals and the financials, greatly favored Brissonneau et Lotz, and were, in fact, eager to see Opel expand its presence beyond the borders of what was then West Germany. And, of course, GM France, a sales and distribution company where I did a stint as head of Sales and Marketing from mid-1966 to late 1968, was more than eager to reap the benefit of the PR boon that would inevitably result from an Opel manufacturing operation in the country.

The German executives, however, were locked into their position of implacable opposition to Brissonneau et Lotz. Some "funny stuff" followed: Karmann submitted a revised bid, accusations were made that the Brissonneau proposal had skipped key steps, such as adequate corrosion protection, etc. All of this noise was easily and quickly dispelled by an eager and highly responsive Brissonneau crew, but new arguments as to "why only Karmann should be considered" surfaced as quickly as prior ones were put to bed.

It became obvious that a decision from the CEO was the only way out of this time-consuming impasse, and thus a substantial meeting was set up in Opel's traditionally furnished historic boardroom. Ralph Mason sat at the head of the huge table and announced that he would hear both sides but, "Bah Gawd," we were going to come out with a decision.

Two massive slide shows followed, one detailing B & L's proposal, the other Karmann's. The bias toward Karmann wasn't too outrageous, so those who favored the French proposal let it go, confident that "the numbers" would carry the day. But then came the big surprise: the total upfront costs of the two bids were shown as equal!

Ralph, obviously having been briefed beforehand, asked to see the breakdown of the two lump sums that had masqueraded as financial data. When the details were exposed, it became clear that the two proposals had been rendered equal by adding $40 million (as I recall) to the

Brissonneau et Lotz proposal for, as the German head of Opel procurement explained, "added travel, need for greater coordination effort, translation, and general inconvenience of dealing with an unknown French supplier."

The decision, for Ralph, was not without risk. What if the Germans, who predicted surefire disaster if the decision went against Karmann, were right? If the program failed, there would be abundant documentation that he had gone against the advice of his German technical people. Ralph cleared his throat, shifted in his chair, and said, "Well, now, that's as big a bunch of bullshit as Ah ever heard! These two proposals both look good, and Brissonneau is way cheaper. And forty million dollars' worth of inconvenience? Hell, Ah don't think so! There's no way on God's earth that you're gonna get forty million of inconvenience. We're going with Brissonneau, and that's it. And Ah won't tolerate foot draggin' or any sabotage. We're all gonna make this work, because it's an important product. Y'all got a choice: get with it or get out! That sufficiently clear to ev'body? Fine! Ah declare this here meetin' to be over!"

Everybody "got with it," and the Opel GT was successfully launched, on time, and with decent quality. In fact, many Opel GTs are in collectors' hands in the United States today.

While Ralph took command and made decisions when they were thrust upon him, his natural lack of real energy ensured that he did not "micromanage" or engage in any real follow-up. In the absence of a good, self-directed team, that could be really detrimental. But in the case of Opel, Ralph was lucky: all of his direct reports were GM's finest, be they the chief designer, chief engineer, controller, or head of manufacturing.

When it became evident that we would have to continue to wait in vain for Ralph to drive the bus, the group took matters in its own hands. Over lunch and in numerous informal meetings, the five or six of us would discuss product and investment strategy. It was totally multifunctional: we all mutually delved into each other's spheres of influence as we sought the optimal way to turn limited resources into great products. A soon-to-retire old U.S. executive, overhearing one of these strategy sessions at lunch, said, "Too many cooks! Too many cooks! We've got the designers talking manufacturing, the finance guy talking chassis, the sales guy talking design. . . . This is crazy! Engineering, and only Engineering, should decide what the future products are going to be."

We disregarded his advice, skimming as it did from the much less competitive '30s, '40s, and '50s, but we did like "Too many cooks," and that name, often abbreviated to "TMC" for purposes of meeting schedules, became our official designation. Design even worked up an embroidered patch featuring chef's hats and crossed wooden spoons, which we affixed to our leisure blazers. The TMC group set its own meeting agendas, resolved conflicts, removed obstacles, and prepared a joint set of recommendations for the mandatory, official product and investment meeting over which the CEO, naturally, had to preside. Not unsurprisingly, these formal meetings were quick and noncontentious. Ralph readily saw the wisdom of what was proposed and intoned, "Well, if that's what y'all agree we should do, and Finance says we got the money and it's all gonna pay back, hell, Ah'm all for it!"

Ralph trusted his team, and in this case, it worked. Clearly, though, the leader who is either too kind or too lazy to probe, follow up, object, or play devil's advocate to ensure he or she is not being sold a bill of goods is skating on thin ice from a personal career perspective, as well as shirking the fiduciary duty to the shareholders.

Fortunately or unfortunately, Ralph and Rina's drunk-scapades must have come to the attention of GM's senior management. In 1971, Ralph was "promoted" out of Opel and elevated to the largely ceremonial post of "chairman, GM Europe," with headquarters in a fashionable part of London. The title would, decades later, actually contain substance. But here, it was a convenient way to get the sodden couple safely out of the way, setting sail on what many at GM referred to as "the sunset cruise." Benevolent old GM never fired failures; it just created a good-sounding job somewhere. Ralph Mason, replaced by the highly energetic, impatient, and hard-hitting Alex Cunningham, was blissfully out of the loop.

Perhaps surprisingly, viewing the Mason tenure at Opel with an unbiased eye reveals a mostly positive assessment: he presided over a remarkable period of design and engineering creativity, turning out cars of advanced design, fine road manners, and great performance. Market share throughout Europe increased, as did profitability. Ralph succeeded despite himself.

5

EBERHARD VON KUENHEIM

CHAIRMAN AND CEO
BMW AG
1970–1993

A Prussian aristocrat with

street-fighter instincts.

FREIHERR (BARON) Eberhard von Kuenheim, born to the German aristocracy, didn't come by his wily willingness to take on any opponent by accident. Born in Juditten, East Prussia, in 1928, he lost his father to a riding accident in 1935. His mother, later captured by the Russian army, died in a Soviet camp shortly after World War II.

Young von Kuenheim stayed a step ahead of the advancing Russian hordes and made his harrowing way to West Germany, where he found family friends and sponsors who gave the young orphan a home and backing. He studied engineering at the renowned Technical University of Stuttgart, an institution that produces a large portion of Germany's formidable technical talent. Graduating in 1954, he soon made a reputation for himself, and in 1959 he was hired into the industrial empire known as the Quandt Group. This massive conglomerate contained such major corporations as Byk-Gulden Chemie, Mauser Small Arms (Jagdwaffen), and, as of 1959, 75 percent ownership of then-troubled BMW. Founder Herbert Quandt saw huge promise in the young baron and, after a series of jobs and ascending responsibility, gave him the helm of BMW in 1970.

I first ran into him at a German auto industry function when he had just been appointed CEO of BMW AG at the youthful age of forty-two. He actually looked even younger:

moderate of stature, sandy hair neatly parted, clear skin on a slightly full face, he had the general appearance of a cleanly scrubbed, well-dressed high school senior ready for his yearbook picture. A small, semipermanent, tight-lipped V-shaped smile did little to dispel the illusion.

We talked superficially about the business and found we could converse easily and liked each other. Little did I realize at the time that this harmless-looking young aristocrat was in the political battle of his life at BMW. The executive VP of sales and marketing, second in command at BMW, bitter at having been passed over for the top job at this late stage of his career, outraged that he was to report to this callow youth, was one Paul Hahnemann. Tall, heavy, outspoken, given to an outrageous sense of humor, Hahnemann had enjoyed a successful career in automotive marketing. His sense for new products was prodigious, and he cleverly exploited niches in the market, essentially creating a class of premium cars just slightly larger than compacts but sold as agile, sporting vehicles at premium prices. These were the BMW 1600, 1800, 2002, and 2002tii, which, with increasing engine size and horsepower, sold at progressively higher prices and were highly profitable.

Accustomed as he was to holding sway at BMW and ignoring a series of weak CEOs, "Nischen-paule" (Niche Pauly), as the adoring media called him, set about undermining von Kuenheim in every way possible. He even routinely introduced his new boss, at both internal and external events, as "our newest, and by far most expensive, apprentice." Von Kuenheim would just smile and gently perform his function.

Underestimating this young baron's intelligence and determination proved to be Hahnemann's undoing. Von Kuenheim, sensing that something "wasn't quite right," launched some focused internal audits, and, to his joy, uncovered massive corruption, with all the ill-gotten gains ending with Hahnemann. Some of it required the collusion of the equally crooked ad agency, which engaged in fictitious billing, a hard-to-spot crime wherein the agency bills the client for media buys that were never purchased. The resulting millions were split between Hahnemann and the agency.

Another scam involved a little-known printing enterprise called Hafis-Verlag. It had 100 percent of the BMW catalog and sales literature business, in all languages, and produced high-quality work but delivered it at outlandish prices. Hahnemann, who insisted that only Hafis could provide BMW with the requisite quality, routinely rebuffed efforts by Purchasing to put the print work out for bids. The audits soon discovered that an attractive woman owned Hafis-Verlag. Further digging revealed her to be Hahnemann's mistress and largely unencumbered with any knowledge of the printing business. In fact, Hahnemann was buying the catalogs from himself: more millions. And on it went: improper kickbacks from foreign distributors in exchange for larger vehicle allocations, "special arrangements" with certain dealers—any and all commonly found corrupt practices that an unethical head of a large sales and marketing department could engage in.

Von Kuenheim nailed him. The baron took all the evidence to the board, many of whose members were aghast that beloved "Nischen-paule" would do such things, and, with the usual corporate desire to avoid embarrassing the company, he was given the boot by "mutual agreement," gave back all or most of the loot, had his reputation intact, and went on to become the head of the German federal railway system. The team at BMW got the message loud and clear: don't be fooled by the frozen smile, the boyish appearance, the soft voice, the cultured accent. . . . This baron is smart and deadly!

And thus it came to pass that I was recruited away from GM to replace Hahnemann. My reputation as a successful sales and marketing practitioner had been well established, and, due to my Swiss birth and upbringing, I would be operating in my native language, although my pronounced Swiss accent would always provide amusement to the natives.

Leaving GM was an easy decision: I was hired away at roughly ten times the annual salary I had at GM, which was admittedly derisory. I would live in the Munich suburbs, with a generous social allowance, two company BMWs, a full-time driver, and a reasonable number of motorcycles. And I was to report to the CEO of a small but prestigious and fast-growing independent auto company, not to the CEO of a subsidiary that reported to a subsidiary, which reported to a regional manager, who reported to the vice president of GM Overseas Operations, who had several more reporting layers separating *him* from the CEO of GM.

All started well, albeit with the first disagreement with my new boss surfacing almost immediately. He called me into his office, which was festooned with foam-backed cardboard panels displaying what was proposed to be the new, much more contemporary, way cooler BMW logo: it was still circular, still with four equal pie slices of alternating white and blue, but devoid of the "old-fashioned" exterior black ring with the three letters "BMW" inscribed upon it.

"I took the initiative upon myself," von Kuenheim explained, "and I commissioned this American firm to come up with some new logo ideas, because the old one stems from the twenties." I was speechless. Here was one of the world's oldest engine companies, fairly recent to car manufacturing, it's true, but recognized the world over for the white-blue whirling propeller, framed by the black ring—a symbol almost worshipped by BMW fans, the object of envy for lesser-valued brands—and now the new CEO wants to make it "cooler."

Mustering all the limited tact I possessed in my tool bag, I explained to him why I thought this was one of the worst ideas ever. He took it all in, never wavering or flinching, and assured me that he would "give it more thought." As anyone familiar with the BMW logo knows, I won that argument. He was gracious in defeat, but my stubborn insistence on the correctness of my views may have been the seminal cause of a sense of unease that was to mark my relationship with the baron from that moment on, although it didn't affect our working relationship initially.

There was much to be done in all areas of the company, but particularly in sales and marketing. Outside of Germany, all vehicle sales, even in common market countries like France, Italy, Benelux, etc., were made through national distributors, who harvested a healthy profit margin from importing BMW cars and motorcycles. In a now largely unified, customs-union Europe, having distributors in lieu of wholly owned BMW sales companies was a costly lapse, and I set out to change it. I had the baron's full support as I battled bribes, threats on my life, offers of Mediterranean yacht cruises with a crew of nubile and guaranteed available females, and in about two years, we got it done, thus vastly improving the profitability of BMW. (He did worry, however, that the financial arrangements with the soon-to-be former distributors were too generous and said I "should have struck better bargains." Perhaps. Hindsight is always the clearest form of vision.)

Another task of major proportions involved the cleanup of the Hahnemann mess. The advertising agency, of course, had to be fired, and a replacement had to be found. It wasn't entirely easy: corrupt though they were, they had, over the years, done a brilliant job of brand positioning.

Most of the folks in Marketing who had been in on the scam had to be fired as well. They and the distribution clerks who pocketed dealer and distributor bribes in exchange for higher vehicle allocations were soon gone, although most honestly believed that there was nothing wrong with what they had done. It was manifestly dishonest by any reasonable standard, but the prevailing culture at the company was such that they were able to construct an elaborate justification for their deeds. I fired them anyway, threats of lawsuits over unjustified dismissal notwithstanding.

With the 1972 Summer Olympic Games soon upon us in Munich, another disagreement loomed with my boss.

Von Kuenheim decided that we would announce our forth-coming all-new 5 Series (midway between the BMW 3 and the large 7) at the Olympics. We in Sales were aghast. Show-ing the prototype next-generation car more than a year be-fore production was to start would seriously crimp sales of the current, aging midsize BMW 1800 and 2000 sedans. In those days, the German public was unaccustomed to model changes. Existing cars were viewed as more or less "perma-nent," and new models would upset the investment that postwar German buyers had made in their cars. Perhaps von Kuenheim was simply ahead of his time. Today, in all regions, new cars are routinely trotted out way before pro-duction, the PR value of the "all new" being deemed well worth the minor effect on current model sales, given a now-jaundiced public.

But at that time, in the spring of 1972, I was dead set against it. Von Kuenheim wouldn't let go, and I wouldn't either. Finally, in a fit of irritation, the baron asked me how I would mark the Olympic occasion, if not with an all-new car. In a flash of inspiration, I said, "Well, let's do what the Americans do: a highly advanced, high-style, radical one-off concept car." He was open to the idea, and Paul Bracq, BMW's gifted but underappreciated head of design, soon delivered sketches of what was to become the groundbreak-ing BMW Turbo Coupe. With its low-silhouette transverse midengine and advanced safety features like radar-controlled braking (all fake and inoperative, as is usually the case with concept cars), it was not only a smash hit, the perfect statement for the Olympics and the generator of dozens of magazine covers, but also the inspiration for John

DeLorean's also-gull-winged, similarly midengine DMC sports car. Happily, von Kuenheim liked what he saw and made it his own. But once again, I had to push and push hard.

Another set of turbulent discussions took place over the proper badging of BMW cars. Back in the 1960s, it was simple: the various body sizes were each equipped with one engine size. Thus, the smallest BMW (abandoned in the '60s) was the 700, its engine size in cubic centimeters. The high-volume sedan was the 1600, and the largest car was the four-door BMW 2000, so named for its two-liter, four-cylinder engine. But the complexity generated by offering larger engines in the smaller cars soon reared its head. What to do when you put the two-liter engine in the 1600? Call it the 1600-2000? The 1600 Two-Liter? That conundrum was resolved by the designation 2002, which became a wildly popular car and perhaps the most iconic BMW ever. Although that fix worked, we could see that the designation system was doomed. With the new midsize BMW sedan (now called 5 Series), we had a real problem, for it was later to be offered with the six-cylinder engine of the large (now 7) series. These were named by their engine size, 2500, 2800, and a slight departure, 3.0. So, what to call a midsize BMW with the 2800 cc six? The 2000-2.8? 2.0-2.8? The organization was churning, trying to find a solution, and the decision deadline for tooling the badges was fast approaching. I was wracking my brain for a logical answer as well, to no avail.

The solution presented itself quietly and unexpectedly in the form of Oskar Kolk, my quietly professional, self-effacing domestic sales manager. He had asked to see me after hours and now sat facing me across the desk. He apologized for the intrusion and explained that all of this really wasn't any of his business, he knew he wasn't in Marketing, that his suggestion probably was worthless, etc. He then unfolded a carefully handwritten sheet upon which, in 100 percent detail, was contained BMW's brilliant model designation, the oldest, clearest, most logical in the industry.

"My thought," Kolk said, "was to call the smaller cars the 3 Series, the midsize ones 5 Series, and the big ones the 7 Series. That would always be the first, identifying digit. The second two digits would connote engine size, so you could have a 316, 318, 320, 325, even a 330 with the big six. The upcoming midsize car would start with the 2-liter four, so it would be the 520. Later, when it gets the 2.5-liter six, it becomes the 525, and nobody would confuse it with the big, current 2500, because that one becomes the 725!"

I loved it. I told him, "Herr Kolk, that's absolutely brilliant! You've solved the problem, and it's solved forever! All I have to do now is get von Kuenheim's blessing, and that should be easy." Kolk, justifiably beaming with pride, left my office. But to my surprise, gaining acceptance for this brilliant naming scheme was to prove a nightmare. Von Kuenheim received it with nods and the usual faint smile, while agreeing ("Ach, ja") that it was clever, intriguing, novel, etc. I soon discovered the reason for the baron's reticence: Dr. Herbert Quandt, the blind owner of 75 percent of BMW, the man who saved the company from liquidation a few years earlier, the chairman of our Supervisory Board, had his own idea for the naming of the new midsize car. It was to be the "BMW 2.0," as von Kuenheim informed me. "Okay," I replied. "But what do we do when it gets a smaller engine or the bigger six? BMW 2.0-2.5? And how will this impact the larger cars? If the big ones ever get a smaller engine, will we call them the BMW 2.5-2.0? With all due respect to the owner, this is silly."

I soon had the opportunity to face Herbert Quandt himself over the issue. Dr. Quandt, sightless eyes pointed vaguely at me, outlined his position: "2.0" sounded important and prestigious and would look good on the car. "But Dr. Quandt," I countered, "think of the confusion resulting from optional engines in the car. What do you do?" He came up with several poorly concocted solutions which I doubt even he thought would work. The good Dr. Quandt, not always a kindly man, was getting irritated: how dare this young Swiss American with the bad accent argue with the de facto owner of the company? I didn't know how I dared, either, but I couldn't help myself. Kolk's proposal was best, would last a long time, and I wasn't going to cave in. Von Kuenheim was no help, making the occasional side comment such as, "Why don't we accept Dr. Quandt's proposal, Mr. Lutz? I'm sure we can find another way to solve the engine size issue."

"Well, no, actually, we can't. We've all tried. Herr Kolk's proposal is the only feasible one. If I didn't believe that, I wouldn't fight so hard." Finally, Dr. Quandt said, "I may be the owner and chairman of the Supervisory Board, but you gentlemen have to run the company. I'm not going to over-rule your recommendation, Mr. Lutz, even though I don't quite like it yet. So I won't stand in the way. Having said that, Mr. Lutz, while I admire your courage and tenacity, I must tell you that you're pushing your luck when you take me on like that. Pushing your luck! Do I make myself clear?"

Choke!! I had just won a battle but had probably forever marked myself as an impertinent, disrespectful, know-it-all smart-ass. "Dr. Quandt," I said, "I didn't mean to offend you, but as your designated head of global sales and marketing, I felt it was my duty to fight for the proposal that I know is best."

The meeting ended, and I felt curiously unelated. BMW's model designation was sold and survives to this day. But von Kuenheim had played his hand perfectly: he had gotten what we all knew was the right decision, but through his extreme willingness to let me do the arguing with Dr. Quandt, it was I who sustained the political losses while he emerged unscathed, his standing with the owner fully intact. It was not the last time I would be seriously outmaneuvered by the wily aristocrat.

Another event occurred in the period post-1972 after BMW displayed the dramatic gull-wing Turbo Coupe as a concept to coincide with the Olympics. Von Kuenheim advised me that we would be taking his chauffeur-driven car from Munich to Stuttgart, not a long trip at 130-mph autobahn speeds. On the way, he briefed me: we were invited to visit with Dr. Joachim Zahn, then the chairman and CEO of Mercedes's parent company, Daimler-Benz AG. No subject had been announced, but von Kuenheim assured me it would be a pleasant meeting. It turned out to undershoot my already low expectations.

Once seated in Dr. Zahn's surprisingly modest conference room, coffee duly served by uniformed staff, the good doctor produced a file containing pictures of the BMW Turbo Coupe concept. "This," he declared, waving the images in my face, "is an outrage! Outrage! BMW has no right to display a gull-wing car! We did that with our magnificent C-111 prototype! You can't do that!"

I asked if Mercedes had a patent or design copyright that we had violated (I knew they didn't, because we had checked) and was told, "That's beside the point! BMW has no right to copy what Mercedes does. Herr von Kuenheim, I want this stopped! Also, Herr Lutz is selling way too many big six-cylinder sedans and coupes. And that must also cease. Six-cylinder cars are *our* specialty! We also do fours, but we agree that's a good field for BMW, as well. You do good fours. Concentrate on those. We'll go easy on fours."

I was speechless. Here was the CEO of our main competitor berating us for competing and not-so-deftly suggesting an illegal market-sharing initiative. *I wonder what the antitrust folks in the United States would think of this conversation,* was the thought that popped into my head. However, in the absence of the SEC or any lawyers, I expected my boss, the baron, to rise to the defense, to express outrage in return, to point out that it was our right and duty to compete fairly, to point out, in no uncertain terms, the impropriety of this whole meeting.

Instead, my disbelieving ears heard something like this: "Of course, Dr. Zahn. Thank you for pointing out these areas of concern. Good relations between our two companies are vital to us both, and we will do nothing to cloud the relationship. I ask you to please excuse Mr. Lutz. He's still fairly new and may have been carried away by enthusiasm in the case of the Turbo Coupe. It wasn't my preferred solution, either. As for sale of six-cylinder cars, we respect Mercedes's preeminence in this area, and we will be careful not to encroach on your territory. Isn't that right, Mr. Lutz?"

I was pretty dumbfounded, and said, "Yes, of course." I had, more or less, been thrown under the bus in the presence of a competitor's CEO.

Later, during the ride back to Munich (I was still fuming, but polite), I remarked how bizarre I had found the meeting, inappropriate, demeaning, and probably illegal even by the relaxed German antitrust standards. My boss said, "Well, don't mind Dr. Zahn. He's old-fashioned about these things, and besides, Herr Flick (a major owner of Mercedes and the founder of Germany's other industrial megaconglomerate) and Dr. Quandt are good friends, so there's nothing to be gained by being confrontational, because the two do compare notes. As for six-cylinder cars, just keep on pushing them."

The lesson for me was that when the chips were down and criticism from outside sources arose, I couldn't count on my boss for backing, even though I thought I had it. This was confirmed by other instances.

There was a luncheon meeting with some distinguished outsider that is emblazoned on my memory. The precise reason I was invited is still a mystery to me. I did not know the guest and was a mere spectator. The invitee was lamenting the continued presence of some high-level executive in his company that he would rather do without, but he was doubtful that he could get the board to support the ouster.

"Aha!" said the baron. "I have a technique: you let this person exercise broad powers and start a lot of initiatives. Some will succeed, and that's good. Some will be controversial or even failures. That, in such cases, is even better. You can pass the failures onto trusted journalists who will run with the story. Leaking enough detail keeps it in the news, and it culminates with speculation that the individual may soon lose his job. At that point, the company says 'no comment!' Soon, the pressure builds to the point where the board feels the need to act, and you're rid of him. So sometimes you need to let the company sustain a little hard times for the greater long-term benefit of getting rid of the undesired executive."

My brain recorded that conversation. Forewarned is forearmed. Although, when I started harvesting negative press coverage for product initiatives gone wrong, the fact that I suspected the source of the "insider information" did me little good in mounting any kind of defense. "Mr. Lutz's failed product initiatives" involved two extroverted, extreme-high-horsepower vehicles which, in normal times, would have been a sensation in the land of unlimited autobahn speeds. One was a heavily modified 2002, with a widened body, huge wheel flares, fat tires, a 200-horsepower (incredible in 1973) turbocharged engine, and a deep front spoiler with the word "Turbo" spelled backward so that sloth-like drivers on the autobahn (those slightly under 100 mph) would read the Day-Glo-enhanced designation in their rearview mirrors and hastily evacuate the left lane.

The other was a lightweight version of the 3-liter coupe, built in a minimum homologation series with all kinds of outlandish front, rear, and roof spoilers, as all the items had to be on a production car in order to be eligible for the prestigious DTM ("Deutsche Tourenwagen Meisterschaft," or "German Touring Car Championship") racing series.

Again, in normal times, these two derivatives would have been hailed as the ultimate street-legal performance cars. Sadly, times weren't normal. The introduction of the nasty duo coincided roughly with the first OPEC oil embargo, which stunned Germany. All of a sudden, wasting fuel by going fast became bad, almost immoral. The Social Democratic government enacted speed limits (greeted enthusiastically by the left), and the media were full of Draconian news of the soon-to-be-permanent energy shortage.

To make matters worse, the nascent green movement in Germany, with the full support of the media, had discovered a phenomenon known as *Waldsterben*, or "dying forests." Indeed, many of Germany's conifers were turning brown and dying. And many coniferous forests had autobahns running through them. In what can be likened to the decades-later human-caused global warming canard, there was soon a scientific consensus among all kinds of semi-qualified pundits that automobile exhaust was to blame. And high speeds meant more exhaust!

This double whammy, delivered by OPEC and the forests, overwhelmed any of the positives of the two high-performance derivatives, and they soon became the poster children for exactly what we must tell the irresponsible auto industry to stop doing. (Some thirty years later, when the Hummer brand became the anti-Christ of the U.S. enviro movement, singled out as perhaps the largest contributor to global warming, despised by Arianna Huffington, attacked from pulpits every Sunday as definitely *not* something Jesus would drive, I was painfully reminded of the BMW 3.0 CSL coupe and the "obruT" 2002. Both are now highly praised collector's items, and *Waldsterben* later turned out to be caused by a bark-boring beetle that makes the rounds every fifty years or so. The media never said, "Oops! Sorry!")

What I lacked in all the furor was any kind of support from BMW's PR machine. It remained silent, except for some interviews with Von Kuenheim, during which he distanced himself from the two cars and described them as "Mr. Lutz's programs." Thanks a lot! I not so fondly remembered the lunch conversation.

As tensions with von Kuenheim mounted, my reaction was counterproductive. Feeling frustrated by my inability to connect with him to honestly discuss our work relationship problems, I took to expressing my feelings and anxiety and frustration to my subordinates and colleagues. While they were sympathetic on the surface, it has to be assumed that much of my negative assessment of his leadership style went right back to von Kuenheim. It no doubt worried him, perhaps even caused him to fear that I was plotting to unseat him. Thus, our relationship, despite major progress in my own career advancement, was trapped in a circularly interactive downward spiral.

One day, in an executive meeting, von Kuenheim casually asked how many old-model unsold coupes were still in company inventory. I said I hadn't checked recently but believed the number to be down to around 200. "I'm shocked that you don't know the exact number, Mr. Lutz. Given the value of those cars, I would assume that you would monitor it daily. I'm the CEO, and even I consider it worth my time. As of this morning, we had precisely 207 in our stock. Please try to exercise a bit more professional diligence, yes?" I was clearly embarrassed in front of my colleagues, who followed the exchange with a mixture of joy ("Glad it's not me!") and compassion. Those who felt the latter knew what von Kuenheim was doing.

The technique of fishing some arcane bit of information out of a subordinate's area of responsibility and then, in front of others, asking him for precisely that number or fact, is a grossly unfair tactic frequently used by bosses who feel the need to keep their direct reports off balance and fearful. It does nothing for healthy cooperation among the individuals who are supposed to be collectively driving revenue and profit.

The baron also seemed ill at ease with senior executives who, with him, were members of the *Vorstand,* or management board. Most were much older, seasoned veterans in their functional fields. It was no doubt hard for the young CEO to drive his agenda against men who both predated him in the company and/or had profound knowledge of their areas of responsibility. So to dodge the pressure, von Kuenheim created a "kitchen cabinet," a group of special assistants to the CEO, one for each functional area, all young graduates of Germany's finest schools, and all tasked with finding out, sleuth-like, what really goes on in Manufacturing, Procurement, Engineering, Sales and Marketing, and so forth. The information gathered went directly to the CEO, and we functional heads knew it and resented it, but were powerless to do anything about it.

A classic example occurred during what was actually a good initiative. Hearing dealers and distributors ceaselessly complaining about the shortage of cars and expressing the worry that we were underproducing to the point where dealers could not be viable in the future, von Kuenheim tasked me with coming up with a five-year "free demand" projection. With only two assembly plants, the aging Munich plant and a new state-of-the-art facility in bucolic Dingolfing, BMW, running flat out with maximum overtime, could produce not quite 200,000 cars, and in the Communist-surrounded Berlin plant, some 20,000 motorcycles. The rise of BMW bikes to six-digit numbers was still some years in the future, but the car production capacity was manifestly inadequate. I was delighted that we were officially acknowledging growth and set both my domestic and my export sales organizations to work canvassing dealers and foreign distributors for their honest, uninflated assessment of demand, year by year, for the next five years.

The total came, not surprisingly to me, to over 500,000 units. At my urging, and so as not to shock the system, we gave the numbers a precautionary haircut to roughly 350,000 per annum after the fifth year. The day of the big presentation saw me talking to a battery of slides, showing demand progression model by model, country by country, year by year, summed up by total domestic, total Europe, total rest of world, and grand total. It was well done and well presented.

I no sooner sat down when von Kuenheim asked his abundantly arrogant young special assistant for Sales and Marketing what he thought of Mr. Lutz's data.

"Freiherr von Kuenheim, my staff and I have been monitoring the development of Mr. Lutz's volume forecast from the beginning. We believe it is preposterously optimistic. And, of course, our main concern is for the BMW brand image: we believe that those volumes would get us perilously close to mass-producer status, and we would lose our carefully nurtured exclusivity. Thus, we recommend that Mr. Lutz's projections be rejected out of hand."

"Well spoken!" said the baron. "Mr. Lutz, BMW must remain BMW . . . small, exclusive, worth waiting for. You are obviously a prisoner of your GM upbringing where more is better. We wish to remain small and precious. Do you understand?"

I could barely control my rage. What the hell, I wondered, had been the point of the exercise? I dreaded facing my own newly optimistic direct reports to tell them that our collective hopes for growth were summarily dashed. (Historical note: despite "small and precious," within five years BMW was producing upward of 350,000 units for sale worldwide, and in 2012, the global sales number was a record 1,540,085 units. And still the BMW image of prestige and aspiration survives!)

I was approaching the last year of my initial three-year contract and was doubtful that it would be renewed. Moreover, I was doubtful that I wanted to spend another three years in such an uncollegial environment, especially with hopes for significant growth seemingly stymied.

Adding to my uncertainty was the fact that the Ford Motor Company was actively recruiting me to be head of Ford of Germany, which, despite the CEO title, was a lesser job than what I currently had. Ford of Germany was a mere badly underperforming sales company in the broader context of the centrally managed, UK-based Ford of Europe.

But the decision, when I finally made it, was surprisingly easy. The so-called crunch point came a few weeks later. It began with a meeting during which Oskar Kolk, my head of domestic sales (and inventor of the 3-5-7 model designation system), came to me with a file on a problematic but large and influential dealer. This retailer had engaged in every imaginable form of fraud at the factory's expense. Whether it was dealer cash for promotions, advertising, or warranty billing, this crook had been stealing us blind, and the evidence was incontrovertible. "Herr Lutz," Oskar Kolk summarized, "this dealer has to be terminated for cause." I agreed. In any relationship between dealers and factory (and customers), integrity is a given.

In view of his importance, I called the dealer in, showed him the evidence, and told him his contract would not be renewed. He silently gathered up his file and departed. That, I assumed, was that! But . . . it wasn't. A few weeks later, the same dealer came to my office, walked up to my desk, and triumphantly slapped his new contract in front of me. It was signed by Eberhard von Kuenheim! Thunderstruck, I asked him how that came about.

"I invited Mr. von Kuenheim to come visit my dealership and he accepted. We had a wonderful lunch and then toured my facility. He was impressed and asked if there was anything he could do for me. I told him I was having a bit of trouble with Messrs. Kolk and Lutz on my new contract, and he said, 'Well, I'll fix that! Give it to me, and I'll sign!' And, as you can see, he did!"

I was apoplectic. An unwritten but widely respected rule is that senior executives do not conduct business with dealers if they are not in Sales, and should, in any and all cases, get a written briefing on the dealer in order to be aware of his strengths and weaknesses. This elementary process had been cheerfully skipped by my boss.

Angrily, I told the dealer, "You wait right here," and stormed down the hall to von Kuenheim's office. Ignoring his secretary, I walked into his office and banged the contract on his desk. "Is this your signature?" I demanded in a tone that conveyed knowledge of the answer. Caught by surprise and visibly shaken, he admitted it, and I proceeded to tell him just how underhanded, improper, and damaging his actions had been. Now visibly agitated, bouncing up and down and waving his shirtsleeved arms, he screamed, "I don't have to account for my actions to you, Mr. Lutz. Not at all! I'm the CEO, and I'll do anything I want to do in Sales or anywhere else! Is that perfectly clear? Now kindly get out of my office!"

That pretty much marked the end of my stay at Bavarian Motor Works. I accepted the offer from Ford, was given a nice send-off party during which von Kuenheim, visibly relieved to be rid of me, heaped praise on me and described me as "unquestionably the best car guy in the industry today." (Unsaid: "Too bad about the other stuff.")

I was determined to hate von Kuenheim for the rest of

my life, but as the years passed and I was, from 1980 to 1985, chairman of Ford of Europe, we often had dinner when he was in London on business. We would talk industry, and he expressed pride in my rise at Ford. He volunteered that my tenacious and ultimately successful efforts to cancel the parasitic importer-distributors in all the large countries, United States included, had been the single most important event in BMW's postwar history, paving the way for profitable global growth. Once, I reminded him of BMW's current volume and contrasted it to the famous "future volumes" meeting and its incomprehensible conclusion. "Yes," he said, "it's so unfortunate that there was so much friction between us. I've often asked myself why. I conclude that we were both too immature, being in our early forties and largely inexperienced. It's a shame, really, but look how well you've done. It fills me with pleasure." He was genuine. I couldn't help liking the older, wiser, more self-confident Freiherr von Kuenheim, and former colleagues at BMW told me that, while still not a model of CEO behavior, he had nonetheless become more open, more sharing, and less Machiavellian.

In the eyes of shareholders, employees, and all the other myriad stakeholders, how good of a CEO was he? In a word: miraculous. He was one of the longest-serving CEOs in automotive history, having held the helm from 1970 to 1993. Leaving the top slot of the management board, he became chairman of the Supervisory Board, a position he held until 1999. He saw his employee base go from 23,000 to more than 80,000. During his tenure, BMW not only became one of the world's three top luxury brands but also successfully resuscitated the iconic Mini brand and, at the other end of the scale, Rolls-Royce.

Thus, while violating many of the traits of a good leader and ruling by secrecy, fear, deft maneuvering, and a sorry lack of trust in his team, the aristocrat-cum-street-fighter has to go down as one of the most successful automotive CEOs of all time, based on the wealth he created for share-holders.

He sent me a heartfelt letter of congratulations on my eightieth birthday. I am, weirdly, proud to have known him.

6

PHILIP CALDWELL

CHAIRMAN AND CEO
FORD MOTOR COMPANY
1980–1985

You might not like him, but

you've got to respect him.

PHIL CALDWELL sat across from me at a small conference table in his office in Ford's world headquarters, the so-called Glass House, in Dearborn, Michigan. He was well tailored in his daily uniform: a densely patterned gray suit, pressed shirt, unobtrusive tie, and carefully shined wing-tip shoes. His face was completely expressionless, which I found disconcerting.

About to depart from my executive VP position at BMW, I had been flown to Dearborn by the then CEO of Ford of Europe, William O. "Bill" Bourke, a gifted and charismatic leader who was to miss his big chance at Ford by being overly candid in his opinion of . . . Philip Caldwell. The first of the Dearborn interviews was with Henry Ford II, shirt-sleeved with dark sweat stains under the armpits. It was an easy conversation; he had been well briefed by Bill Bourke. Despite the legendary power he wielded in the company, I found him charming and not intimidating in the slightest.

That meeting was followed by one in Lee Iacocca's office, which wasn't so much an interview as it was a stream of consciousness by the flamboyantly dressed Lido, now Ford president, delivered after offering me a genuine Monte-cristo "Especial" from his personal humidor. Puffing on his, he covered a wide range of topics in his rambling speech, including the fact that he had checked me out with his buddy Elliott "Pete" Estes, president of GM, to see if they would have wanted me back (the answer was yes), that he was disappointed Bill Bourke hadn't "fixed" Ford of Germany yet, that I had better get in there and kick some butt to save Bill's, and many other semirelated topics. It was, as usual with Iacocca, a motivating, if lopsided, conversation.

Coming off of these two successful interviews, I expected the one with Phil Caldwell, executive VP of International Operations and thus Bill Bourke's boss, to be a mere courtesy, an easy "welcome aboard." But unlike the preceding interviews, this one was tense and Bill Bourke was excluded. It was strictly one-on-one.

After staring at me intently for what seemed like an eternity, Phil, without any preamble, asked, "So, why are you leaving BMW?" Without criticizing von Kuenheim, I explained that there were differences in philosophy that had strained the relationship, that the company was small, and that I missed the order, predictability, rationality, and freedom from corruption that marked GM and Ford. Caldwell probed, and I stated that it mostly had to do with my frustration over a lack of growth strategy at BMW.

No smile from Caldwell. No flicker of an eyelid. Just that same immobile, neutral poker face. After another pregnant pause, Caldwell asked, "So, why did you leave General Motors?" Again, trying to avoid criticism of a former employer, I said, truthfully, that I had been recruited for the BMW job at a multiple of my GM compensation. Stone-faced again, "So, why do you want to work for Ford, and what do you think you can bring to the party?" That was followed by "Why did you select UC Berkeley?" and "What did you do in the Marine Corps?"

With the absence of any visual change in body language or verbal acknowledgments, the whole conversation seemed strange and devoid of any "chemistry." I was, however, hired, and despite spending much time with Phil Caldwell, in groups as well as one-on-one, the feeling of unease in his presence never left me.

Caldwell was born in 1920 in Bourneville, Ohio. His parents were farmers. He graduated from Muskingum College in 1940, Harvard Business School in 1942, and served as a lieutenant in the navy until the end of the war. He was fond, when in his rare expansive moods, of telling his audience how "General Douglas MacArthur and I" had fought the Japanese, undoubtedly a generous assessment of his own role, although it is theoretically possible that he actually had met the general and had served on his staff as a junior logistics officer.

Joining Ford in 1953, Phil Caldwell headed Truck Operations, the ill-fated Philco appliance division, and, when I met him, International Operations. Perhaps the best description of Phil Caldwell came from the lips of Henry Ford II's butler in the Ford apartment, flat 121 in the Grosvenor House in London. When not used by Mr. Ford, the luxurious, multiroomed apartment was available to executives at the officer level. Bedwell, the butler (butlers in the UK are always called by their last names), was serving me one evening after he had just come off a full week of attending to the needs of Phil Caldwell. "I beg your pardon, sir, but may I ask you something?" "Sure!" "Well, sir, I always try to please, and consider myself an excellent professional, but I must say, Mr. Lutz, that I find Mr. Caldwell to be a highly unusual person." That phrase, or versions of it, would be repeated to me by literally dozens of people who felt diminished by their encounter with Caldwell and wanted to talk about it.

In the case of Bedwell, it involved Caldwell's freshly shined shoes, which he held under Bedwell's nose and asked, "Bedwell, what do you see wrong with these?"

"Nothing, sir. I see a properly polished pair of shoes, sir."

"Look again, Bedwell. Look closely."

"I don't see anything, sir."

"Well, I'll give you a clue: they're not even!"

"Not even, sir? Could you tell me what's not even?"

"The laces, Bedwell. The laces. They're not exactly the same length."

Bedwell took the shoes, evened up the laces, and brought them back. He told me that in his many years of service to Henry Ford II, and with the royal household before that, he had never had such an experience. I told him Phil Caldwell was a fine executive and that we all had to overlook some of his major personal idiosyncrasies.

One time, my regular chauffeur at Ford had left me to my own devices in order to drive Phil Caldwell during one of his visits to Germany. Returning to my service, he said, "May I say something about Mr. Caldwell, sir?" "Sure, go ahead," I replied. It seems my driver had been told by Caldwell to seek out the manager (not an assistant manager) at the hotel where Caldwell stayed. The manager would give him a zipper bag of highly confidential content. He was to take the bag directly to the General Aviation terminal at the Bonn airport, find the captain of the Ford Air Gulfstream IV, and deliver the secret bag. My driver had to insist at the hotel before they actually produced the manager, who, nodding knowingly, duly produced the heavy zipper bag. Probably trembling with excitement and feeling a bit like a secret agent, the driver took it to the airport and found the pilot. The latter, quite used to such situations, apparently said, "Okay, leave it on the bench. I'll take it out to the plane later." Horrified, the good chauffeur said, "Oh, no, Mr. Caldwell said it's very important that the bag be placed on the airplane at once. We can't leave it anywhere!" At this, the pilot said, "Aw, fer Chrissake! I'll show you what's in the damn bag," and, so saying, yanked open the zipper to the shock of the designated courier. There, for all to see, was a cloth airline bag overflowing with dozens of the tiny little jam pots that were routinely served with breakfast at the better European hotels! So much for the top-secret highly important mission.

Another time, a Ford flight attendant (I was the only passenger) asked if it was okay to ask me about Mr. Caldwell. "Sure," I said, "let's hear your story." It seems she was once on a long flight with Phil. He was the only passenger. She needed a smoke and, screwing up her courage, asked if he would mind if she went to the very back of the plane for a cigarette. Phil thought for a while and then said, "I disapprove of your smoking, but I can understand your nicotine dependency. I would never do anything to compromise safety or diminish your ability to perform your duty in case of emergency. Therefore, in the interest of flight safety, go have a cigarette." Needless to say, the flight attendant decided she didn't "need" a cigarette.

Phil Caldwell and his wife, Betsy, were teetotalers. No wine, spirits, beer, coffee, or tea. No intoxicants and no stimulants. Nothing but water. The absence of drinking was a source of bemusement to Henry Ford II, who drank more than moderately. At one company function, Henry Ford II tried to induce Phil to have just a tiny taste of wine. Phil declined, saying he and Betsy touched no alcohol. Somewhat frustrated and moderately drunk, Mr. Ford loudly said, "Hell, Phil, I don't get it. You don't smoke, you don't swear, you don't drink, you don't take coffee or tea. . . . What the hell *do* you do?" It was a good question!

I got used to Phil Caldwell's disdain for alcohol. Whenever we were on a plane or eating in a restaurant and the server asked about a predinner cocktail, Phil always demurred. I would then politely ask, "Is it okay if I order one, Phil?" His answer, unfailingly, was, "Go right ahead if you feel you need it." The effect, the first time, was similar to that for the smoking flight attendant: I no longer wanted the drink since I didn't want to appear an addict. Later, I decided I would have the drink, and when my polite question received the same reply, I said, "It's not a question of need, Phil. I just would like one."

Mr. Caldwell was great at maintaining an image of himself that did not correspond, quite, to the underlying reality. Once, I had a lengthy bout of tendinitis in my right elbow which made it extremely painful to shake hands. Caldwell and I were in Henry Ford's office when I offered my left hand as Mr. Ford greeted me. He talked about my condition for a few minutes, suggested a doctor (who actually later cured it), and warned me to take it easy. At the end of the meeting, I picked up my briefcase, which was not a pain-inducing activity. To my surprise, Phil Caldwell leaped to my side and grabbed the case. "I don't want you carrying anything; we've got to heal that elbow!" He wouldn't heed my protests and lugged both my briefcase and his. I'm sure Henry Ford II was impressed that this very senior officer showed such concern for the health of one of his juniors. Too bad Mr. Ford didn't see the scene in the corridor as we exited his office. No sooner was the door closed than Caldwell coldly handed me my briefcase with the words, "Here. You take it!" Curiously, the fact that he performed these little acts of intellectual dishonesty in front of people who would remember them didn't seem to bother Phil in the slightest.

Once, at the quarterly European Automotive Operations review meeting in London, he called me to his side of the conference table. As I knelt by his side, he whispered instructions in my ear. I'm certain the other meeting participants thought that I was privy to some really special message. But that was not the case. It seems that Phil Caldwell, when in the UK, became enamored of Cussons Imperial Leather soap, an expensive and elegantly presented cleansing product. My mission: go to the maitre d' of the No. 4 Grafton Street townhouse, owned by the company and the venue of the meeting, and have him give me a twenty-four pack. Said batch of expensive soap was to be shielded in brown wrapping paper and securely tied with string for easy handling. I duly left the meeting and passed the request on to Neil, the maitre d', who shrugged his shoulders, registered no surprise, and set about making the package. When it was ready, a secretary brought me a note thus informing me. I left the meeting, got the large brown package from Neil, took it into the meeting room, and set it down next to Phil's chair. He acknowledged it with a solemn nod, conveying both shared wisdom and awareness of the importance of the mission. By now, I'd figured out that Phil liked free stuff.

One of Caldwell's other idiosyncrasies concerned an English product by the name of Malvern Water. This bottled beverage came in a traditional tall glass bottle, and it was his beverage of choice. He insisted on having it everywhere, and the company plane always had to be amply stocked. Once, after he completed a three-week trip through the Far East, drinking locally unavailable Malvern Water the whole time, I asked one of the flight attendants (the smoker) how they could possibly have had that many bottles on the G-IV. "We only had four bottles of his damn water," she said. "When they were empty, we refilled them with whatever!"

Then there was the Malvern Water incident in Brazil, which nearly took a dramatic turn. Lynn Halstead, VP for Latin American Operations, was hosting a major business dinner in honor of the visiting Phil Caldwell at São Paulo's exclusive Jockey Club. Phil wanted his Malvern Water, and Lynn had taken pains to ensure an adequate supply, getting several bottles to the Jockey Club before the event. The time approached for beverages. Lynn and the executives and guests were poured an excellent crisp Brazilian white wine. Phil was proffered . . . wait! What's this? A napkin-wrapped silver pitcher! "No, no!" said Phil. "I want my Malvern Water." The headwaiter came over to see if he could quell the growing disturbance. "Sir, that *is* your Malvern Water. It's in the pitcher. We always decant the water into frosted pitchers. We find it more elegant. But I assure you, it is your Malvern Water." Phil wasn't buying it. "I want my Malvern Water, and I want it in the original bottle. Is that clear?" At this point, Lynn Halstead got active. He told the headwaiter to comply. By then, the club manager intervened and told Lynn, now a safe distance from the table, that he didn't give a damn who Caldwell was, he was not going to put water bottles on the table. "Besides," he said, "I give you my word that that was his Malvern Water in that pitcher. By refusing it, he is questioning my integrity. I won't stand for it!"

Lynn did the right thing: he gave the manager a major tune-up, stressing again the supreme importance of Phil Caldwell and reminding the manager just how much business the Jockey Club got from Ford. "You and I have been friends and have done a lot of business. Now do me this one favor: get the man his Malvern Water bottle." Defeated, the manager complied. Phil triumphantly poured from his own, very special bottle. He was content and drank the whole bottle. Lynn later thanked the manager for his understanding and thoughtfulness. "It was easy," he replied. "In fact, I enjoyed it. I poured his Malvern Water out of the pitcher and down the drain and filled the Malvern bottle with our 'special' Brazilian tap water."

Sadly, Phil's insistence on absolute obedience at times took bizarre twists: Ford of Europe had successfully launched the subcompact Fiesta in 1977, and it was now time to kick off the design and engineering of the 1981 Escort, a modern, front-wheel-drive compact, a size larger than the Fiesta. Phil had decreed that the same platform (essentially, the chassis of a modern car, which also sets up length and width) be used for the Escort. We knew it wouldn't work. The subcompacts, to European eyes (and, most recently, to American ones as well), were a whole lot smaller than the compact cars, and the former could not possibly masquerade as the latter. We attempted to explain this, but to no avail. Finally, after a particularly arduous session, Phil agreed that the planned 1981 Escort could be a "stretched" Fiesta. That, at least, solved the problem of the missing length, but the resulting car would still lack the requisite width, and, as the late, great Bill Mitchell, VP of Design at GM, liked to say, it would "look like it was designed in a narrow hallway."

Well, I thought, we have half a loaf. Then, the Ford of Europe VP of Engineering spoke up. "Phil, while we're doing the stretch, I think we could also widen it!" Since this is manifestly impossible if the same platform is to be used, I was expecting Phil to say, "What are you trying to pull? 'Stretch and widen' means a new underbody, and that's what I'm asking you to save." Instead, he beamed at the VP and said, "Now we're getting to the intelligent solution! Stretch and widen the Fiesta platform; that's the way to go!"

To my utter amazement, we had just sold the needed size for the Escort! It would never again be referred to as a "new underbody"; instead, it was religiously and consistently called a "stretched and widened Fiesta." And so that we weren't completely dishonest, there was about a three-foot section of the floor pan that had exactly the same shape as the Fiesta. Thus, Fiesta DNA was alive and well, we had the car we needed, no money was saved, and Phil Caldwell went away with the warm feeling that, thanks to his leadership, major subcompact/compact commonality had been achieved, generating as yet unfathomed engineering and manufacturing efficiencies. It was "refilled Malvern Water bottles" all over again.

The 1981 Ford Escort, when introduced, was elected European Car of the Year and, together with its U.S. counterpart of the same name (similar, but no common parts), became the best-selling car in the world.

Phil was not one to throw in the towel in discussions. I recall a marathon session in the Ford of Europe conference room when we were seeking his endorsement of the Cargo truck program, an all-new medium-to-heavy vehicle for Europe to replace the venerable Ford D series—a common, if unexciting, workhorse—especially in the British market.

I delivered the presentation, which, with ensuing discussion, was to fill a two-hour time slot from 2:00 to 4:00 P.M. We had not counted on Phil's near-insatiable appetite for detail, as well as his manifest need to be perceived as a major expert in the commercial vehicle field, since it had once been under his leadership. I couldn't get through the presentation, being constantly stopped. Are those the main competitors? Why? Why not others? Why do customers buy theirs and not ours? What are the competitors' horsepower, payloads, and reliability ratings? Why would anybody want our truck? Could we do an even larger version? How much commonality between the regular cab and the long-haul "sleeper" cab? Why not more? How much commonality do the competitors have? Why do we have less/more? Why a UK plant? Why not Portugal? And on, and on, and on. Four P.M. came and went. The remaining presenters scheduled to follow me were sent home while Phil drilled through strata upon strata of my then-considerable knowledge of what we were doing, why, and against whom. Phil and the senior management group were to meet in a renowned London restaurant at 6:30. The time came and went, as Phil relentlessly bombarded me with ever more arcane questions. Finally, at 6:50, there was a reminder that we had a formal dinner reservation. Phil Caldwell reluctantly declared a truce and said we would continue this vital dialogue some other time (which, mercifully, never came about. The Cargo truck program continued to fruition and was, in a very tough competitive battlefield, moderately successful).

As we exited the paper-strewn conference room, I brought up the rear. I was a bit shell-shocked, not knowing if I had done well or had failed—as usual with Phil, verbal feedback and body language were both ultraneutral. As I prepared to leave the room, I was stopped by one Chalmers Goyert, personal assistant to Henry Ford II and often his surrogate observer in meetings. Mr. Ford, for whatever reason, could not attend. Chalmers had silently witnessed the afternoon performance. He faced me squarely, paused for a moment, and said slowly, "The greatest fool in the world can ask questions the wisest man can't answer. Let's go to dinner." I felt better! It was hard to judge whether Phil Caldwell liked me, had any respect for my performance, or simply tolerated me because I was, undeniably, an executive vice president.

From time to time, Phil would invite me to his Glass House office for a chat. These discourses, for the conversation was heavily one way, usually came at the end of a busy day and lasted from 5:00 to 7:00 P.M. It was not uncommon for Phil to begin with his military experience, frequently dropping the name of MacArthur. He would go on to outline, in some detail, the "special trust and confidence" bestowed on commissioned officers, and how this obligated them to a set of ethics, rules, codes of conduct. I agreed. But, invariably, at the end of the monologue, Phil would look at me and say, "But you wouldn't understand, because you never served." At that point, I always said, "Well, as you know, Phil, I spent five years on active duty in the Marine Corps, was a jet aviator, plus another six years flying with the reserves. I held the rank of captain." This failed to faze him, and he'd continue to explain whatever point he was making to my hopelessly nonmilitary mind.

It was during the Caldwell administration that the giant consulting firm of McKinsey and Company was called in to diagnose and, hopefully, rejuvenate some of the Ford Motor Company's tortuous decision-making and approval processes. The intellectual firepower and the sheer chutzpah of Ford's formidable finance group (a creation of the legendary Ed Lundy, one of the original "Whiz Kids") had created such an airtight network of preanalysis, analysis, and postanalysis that initiative was stifled, making it difficult for the operating people to get anything done. It felt like we were running a foot race in twelve inches of solidifying concrete.

The intrepid consultants interviewed dozens, if not hundreds, of executives and basically always heard the same refrain: the hegemony of Finance is slowing things down. My contacts at McKinsey assured me that this would change for the better. Months (and millions) later, the grand overhaul was announced: the much-reviled Finance group was untouched, but now they faced what was billed as a "counterbalance" in the form of a brand-new "Corporate Strategy and Analysis" staff (CSA for short), which would report to the CEO.

The announcement did not generate the hoped-for enthusiasm: instead of dealing with only one set of highly analytical bean counters, we now faced two! But there was a difference: where Finance would focus on the grimly numerical dissection of the short and medium term, CSA would turn its quantitative laser beam on the long-term strategy of all areas of the company.

The reader may recall that, in the early 1980s, it was a generally held consulting company finding that American companies need to do more highly detailed long-range planning. I was, and am, a skeptic: in a highly volatile technological, political, regulatory, and economic environment, where is there value in precisely defined business strategies ten years out when we barely have visibility for the next twelve to fifteen months? Why waste time on overdefining a future that we know won't occur? My protests fell on deaf ears.

But Phil Caldwell loved it. He could now do what visionary CEOs are supposed to do: set their gaze over the horizon, and chart a new course! Many hours of meeting time were squandered as function after function presented overly precise, single-scenario descriptions of where and what they would be ten years hence. As an executive vice president, I had to sit through days of soporific meetings devoted to the long-term future.

Things came to a head in a long-range product planning meeting in which the discussion centered on the *precise* requirements (size, weight, cost, performance) of the Ford Escort . . . two generations out. I sat next to Phil, on his left, listening to various factions arguing about millimeters of rear legroom on cars we wouldn't even begin planning for seven more years.

I doodled, and slowly smoked a then-permissible cigar.

Phil turned to me and in front of the assembled conference table said, "You're obviously not paying attention, Bob. Are we boring you?" I replied, "Phil, with all due respect, this is wasted effort. The car we're talking about doesn't need to be defined for another seven years. We've got one whole generation ahead of it. We don't know what fuel prices, regulations, or competitor models will be in place by then. What if Volkswagen introduces a huge Golf six years from now and it's a runaway success? Won't we base our dimensional targets on that? I just can't see planning things years before we have to plan them; that's my problem here!"

Phil drew himself up, pursed his lips in a blend of astonishment and disapproval, turned to the assembled executives, and slowly said, "Well, when we got rid of Iacocca, I thought we had rid ourselves of the last of the hip shooters. Unfortunately, I now see that that is not the case!" It was clearly not a career-enhancing moment.

Looking at the sum of these vignettes of Phil Caldwell's senior management tenure, it would be tempting to dismiss him as a sort of corporate Captain Queeg: petty, focused on personal prestige, uncaring about his subordinates, and given to poor business judgment. In short, not the type of personality one would want to guide the fortunes of what was then the second-largest car company in the world.

But surprisingly, that would be the wrong conclusion. While lacking any real operational or "car guy" interests, or skills, for that matter, and being consistently overly passionate about getting more data to support eminently logical decisions, Phil Caldwell had one powerful sense of purpose that overrode his many quirks and foibles: he was totally, undeviatingly focused on making Ford the quality leader of the world, surpassing the then seemingly unbeatable Toyota. He teetered on obsession. But when it came to quality in the United States, it took an obsessive personality to energize a culture raised on "nobody's perfect, and good enough is fine" or "all we have to achieve in quality is the same level as GM."

Phil cut through that in his usual stubborn, unreasonable, step-by-step, "peel the onion one layer at a time" way. When it was "See, Phil, the Japanese have higher-quality suppliers," he said, "Well, get the same suppliers, or have them form joint ventures with their U.S. counterparts." That got done, just as excuse after excuse was annihilated under the slow, inexorable weight of Phil Caldwell's steam-roller. Often reminded of the perilous financial position in which Ford found itself at the time (Chrysler had basically gone under and was seeking federal loan guarantee relief) and warned that his quality obsession was costing a lot of money, Phil was wont to say, "We may go out of business. I hope we don't, but if we do, I want people to say, 'What a shame! They were building the best cars and trucks in the world!' "

Phil was a strong supporter of compelling products and pushed heavily for advanced European designs. He had re-alized that American taste was rapidly shifting away from traditional, glitzy, boxy, vinyl-roofed styling and was more and more drawn to the sleek, functional aesthetics as exem-plified by German makes such as Audi and BMW.

Consequently, he became the leading supporter of the original Taurus-Sable twins: sleek, aerodynamic midsize se-dans unlike anything ever produced in the United States. I personally "helped" with that direction, even though, as head of International Operations, I had, strictly speaking, no business getting involved with a strictly domestic U.S. program. I met many times with Jack Telnack, the coura-geous and exceptionally talented Ford chief designer at the time. The Taurus and Sable, we decided, had to be basically an American version of the large Audi 5000 (possibly still called "Audi 200" at that time), which we both considered to be the personification of the future, aerodynamically ef-ficient passenger car. Don Petersen, then president and designated successor to Phil Caldwell, was also heavily in favor of the Taurus program. The only high-level detractor was the late Harold A. "Red" Poling, then in charge of Ford's North American Operations. (In the Poling obituaries, he is credited with the Taurus. In truth, it happened despite his bitter opposition. More about that in the next chapter.)

Phil Caldwell referred to Taurus and Sable as "our silver bullets," because the clay models in Design were painted in a bright, metallic silver. Phil was right about their future impact on Ford, and the introduction of the two wildly successful vehicles coincided with the end of his tenure. Things were beginning to look much better for the Ford Motor Company and its shareholders.

So here we have a senior leader, grandiose and petty at the same time. A man of great talent, yet beset by "imposter syndrome," a condition wherein the victim can hardly believe that his poor, pathetic, underexperienced self has actually attained this highest rank possible. The insistence on deference, privilege, and right to "office supplies" helps remind the sufferer that, yes, it's really him! Everyone contracts this perfectly normal affliction at some state in their lives. The trick is to remind yourself that, imperfect and undertrained as you may know yourself to be, there's a reason they picked you: you're less imperfect and less undertrained than the others they considered and rejected.

Phil Caldwell was great but also immensely flawed. Here is an anecdote that perhaps best sums up this hugely complex man.

Phil had me in his office for one of his after-hours "Bob Lutz mentoring sessions," as described previously. I routinely dreaded these and was always on my guard, taut as a banjo string, because while we talked for two hours, I never felt any genuine intellectual connection. Phil, despite his long-winded homilies, remained sphinxlike. But this one session was different. After a while, Phil fell silent as if mulling a thought. Then he said, "I'm going to show you something that not many people have seen." With that, he reached into the credenza behind his desk and withdrew a heavy, dark maroon leather-bound album. It contained page upon page of pictures of Philip Caldwell in the presence of heads of state, princes, kings, sheiks, Chinese ministers and vice chairmen, notables from the worlds of politics, science, royalty, and show business. It was fascinating.

Then, when show-and-tell was over and he ceremoniously closed the heavy book, my eyes fell on the gold embossed title. Suddenly, I understood Phil Caldwell, his hopes, dreams, grandeur, and weakness, all brilliantly encapsulated in one simple phrase. It read: "Important People Who Have Met Me."

7

HAROLD A. "RED" POLING

CHAIRMAN AND CEO
FORD MOTOR COMPANY
1990–1993

The bean counter's bean
counter. If it can't be quantified,
I don't want to know about it.

IT WAS in the summer of 1974 that I made the move from executive vice president of Sales and Marketing at BMW in Munich to managing director of Ford of Germany. On paper, it sounded grandiose; a move from the tier just under Eberhard von Kuenheim to actually running a car company in Germany. But I well knew that the reality was different: Ford of Germany (FOG) had once been proudly independent like its sister company Ford of Britain (FOB) and produced its own full line of cars with its own engineers, manufacturing staff, finance staff, procurement, etc. It worked from the 1930s through the early 1960s. But the minimum scale for a successful car company was getting bigger by leaps and bounds, and Henry Ford II, ever the visionary, saw that the various independent Ford operations in Europe had to be consolidated into one efficient, pan-European operation. After much organizational hand-wringing and predictions of doom and corporate devastation, Ford of Europe was set up in Brentwood, Essex, near London. The UK was picked because this new entity was to require dozens of senior U.S. corporate personnel, and it was considered important that the accompanying spouses be able to conduct their lives in something resembling their natural tongue. Naturally, the Germans saw the new headquarters location as a defeat only slightly less catastrophic than the loss of World War II, and they feared that many future decisions would now inevitably favor the Brits. Seeing as the teeming thousands of Ford of Europe staff positions were given to well-educated, articulate, and politically savvy Englishmen, their fears were not without considerable foundation, and Warley (the small town near Brentwood where the headquarters was actually located) became a four-letter word at Ford of Germany.

Nevertheless, the concept was correct: central finance coordinated all the cost, investment, and accounting activities for both FOG and FOB. Manufacturing was centralized, as was engineering, with portions of the new, jointly designed and engineered cars created in Germany, others in the UK, which led to the comical sight of dozens of engineers commuting between Cologne and Stansted (UK) on the corporate BAC-III airliners with instrument panels, grilles, front fenders, and suspension parts as carry-on luggage.

The only functions that were not actually run (gut-guided, monitored, checked, and recommended) by Ford of Europe were Sales, Marketing, Public Relations, and Government Relations. I was to oversee these departments, but German corporate law demanded that the CEO of Ford of Germany actually have the *Vorstand* (management board) report to him. Thus, I had "legal" responsibility for all aspects of the largely fictitious German entity, and dutifully held my weekly *Vorstand* meetings, in which almost every member actually reported to an American executive in Warley! It was a challenging situation, but one for which I was ideally suited: with my Swiss background, my BMW experience, and my native German language ability, I was accepted in Germany as one of their own. Similarly, my U.S. background and GM experience, combined with my undeniable English language skills, gave me credibility in Warley, where I was never considered to be one of the whiny Germans perennially dissatisfied with Warley and centralized control. I was, in a sense, the cultural bridge, and it worked to everyone's advantage. I grew very adept at my role of pretending, vis-à-vis the German media and government, that I was in charge of everything, including the difficult area of labor relations, when, in fact, I had little say in anything other than my official Sales, Marketing, PR, and Government Relations function.

Harold A. "Red" Poling was CFO of Ford of Europe when I arrived, and my CFO of Ford of Germany had already advised me that his real superior in Warley was one tough SOB and not easy to deal with.

Red had an excellent early career at Ford in the United States, serving as controller in the Steel Division, Transmission and Chassis Division, Engine Division, and, finally, Ford North America Product Development. He was justifiably proud of the fact that all of his assignments had been in *operational* finance jobs, not in the (for him) comfortable ivory-tower world of corporate finance. No question about it: Red Poling knew, intimately and by hands-on experience, how the car business runs. Somewhat unfortunately, though, his vast experience meant that he saw it as a hugely complex set of numbers and line-item budget elements.

On my first day at the FOG office building in Cologne, I was duly deposited by my chauffeur in a fairly nasty UK-designed Ford Granada (no relation to the equally pathetic

U.S. car of the same name). It was a clear comedown from the superb 3-liter BMW sedan which had served as my chauffeured conveyance for the previous three years.

But if the car was a letdown, my CEO office served to demoralize me completely. The carpet was Ford standard gray utility, basically designed for hallways in plants or other high-use areas. Nothing wrong with that, except for the two huge, gaping holes in the center, through which peeked worn linoleum. The desk was a massive light-tan wooden affair, chipped and missing both corners as well as some drawer pulls. The radiator covers also were massive wooden affairs, heavy ash or oak with slots at the top. But the conference table and chairs were even worse. The whole thing was brought into a sort of dismal focus by a shabby ficus tree, largely bereft of foliage.

I expressed amazement to the FOG head of General Services (who did not really report to me) and asked how I could possibly greet important visitors, dealers, suppliers, and media people in such a rat hole. He agreed. A project was put together for a desk, furniture, carpeting, and desk accessories and submitted to Ford of Europe. It wasn't lavish; my memory serves up $15,000 (1975 dollars, of course; multiply by three for today's cost). Silence ensued until the arrival in my office of an affable young executive, who introduced himself as Gerry Greenwald, head of General Services, Ford of Europe.

"I'm here because Red doesn't believe this office needs fixing up. He hates office refurbishments. Actually, other than the carpeting, this doesn't look bad at all. Certainly up to Ford corporate standard. I'm sure we have some of that gray carpet; it's Ford standard, too. We'll cut out some larger sections and replace where the holes are." "Gerry," I said, "are you nuts? I have to receive visitors here! What kind of impression does this make?"

Gerry gave a "not my worry" shrug, and I escorted him out. I was furious, and called my head of General Services. "I knew this would happen," he said. "You know, they don't mind spending a load of money putting Greenwald on the corporate plane, but they won't approve a logical, simple project. Let me see if I have any flexibility with the maintenance budget. Leave it to me!"

Shortly thereafter, I departed on a weeklong trip to the United States. When I returned and entered my outer office, I was met by my beaming secretary. She ushered me into an office I didn't recognize in the location where mine had been. The desk was now flat black but topped with brushed stainless steel. The same material covered the ugly radiator shrouds, which now took on a distinctly high-tech aura. The carpet was a gorgeous apple green with a close-shorn nap. The conference table was a thick slab of glass, perched on four chrome-plated cylinders. The far wall was in a complementary darker green while the wall to the right was covered in smooth, dark brown cork. Beautifully centered was a framed designer's rendering of a futuristic Ford midengine sports car.

I was stunned and called the General Services guy. "How did this happen?" I asked, afraid I had triggered an illegal act. "Don't worry, sir. It's all on the maintenance budget. I called the Design guys (also not my "real" direct reports), and they agreed that it was a point of pride for them to have their symbolic CEO in a halfway decent office, so they designed it and furnished all the materials. The desk isn't new, it's just completely redone. We actually loved doing it. Sort of a finger in the eye of Ford of Europe, if you get my drift."

The green carpet, of course, was new and had cost DM400. I reimbursed the company for the roughly $200 outlay—wisely, it turned out, because on his next visit, the ever-vigilant Gerry Greenwald, flabbergasted, asked, "Where the hell did all this come from?" "Normal maintenance, Gerry, and here's the receipt for the carpet. You can deny my project, but you can't force me to work and receive VIPs in a shit house!"

(Gerry was basically a good executive. After a stunning career failure as CEO of Ford of Venezuela, he was picked up by Lee Iacocca, then CEO of Chrysler, and named chief financial officer. Later, he became CEO of Chrysler Motors, a division of the Chrysler Corporation, headed, of course, by Iacocca. In 1986, when I joined Chrysler, I reported to Gerry, and it was a productive relationship.)

The office experience was my introduction to the world according to Poling: no project too trivial to be questioned, no cost too low to be given a 20 percent cut, no outlay sufficiently justified to not be closely investigated for padding or outright deceit. It was financial micromanagement at its absolute worst. The tragedy of this type of bean-counter-ism is that, besides applying the brakes to progress and being thoroughly demoralizing, it actually drives hidden waste and cost . . . cost spent investigating, cost spent rejustifying, and cost driven by the clever troops (like my General Services manager) finding an alternate, far more expensive way to get the job done, but using the subterfuge of dipping into various approved budget line items to avoid having to submit anything to higher authority.

My next lesson from "Poling Land" came in the spring of 1976. The budget called for a 4.3 percent across-the-board price increase; it was routine in the Federal Republic at the time. Also routine was the unwritten agreement with the (then Socialist) government and the other automobile companies that prices were to be raised *after* completion of the annual wage negotiation with Germany's powerful metalworking union, the IG Metall. The belief was that in so doing, we could claim that wages drove pricing, not vice versa, as the union claimed.

The trouble in 1976 was that the normally quickly concluded wage round (the Employers' Federation, not the individual companies, did the bargaining) was dragging on and on, and passed the budgeted price increase date. Poling was furious and demanded to know why I hadn't priced. I explained, repeatedly, in person, on the phone, and in memos, that the government and media reaction to pricing ahead of the wage increase outcome would be devastating. It would even, I argued, risk the union then asking for even more. (That duly came to pass, and my fellow German CEOs in the car and metalworking industries quite naturally blamed me for it.)

Poling was unmoved. "I can show you the daily aggregate loss of profit for FOG for each day you delay pricing. Tell you what: you show *me* an analysis, a hard analysis, not an 'I think' one, of how much pissing off the government and the media will cost, and maybe I'll listen." Compelled by honesty and realism, I told him that it would be a guess, because there was no precedent: no company had ever violated the unwritten rule. "In that case," Poling countered, "you'll price before the end of the week!" And I did.

I've never had trouble accepting praise for something successful that was only partly my doing. Now I got a dose of accepting massive blame for doing something I had bitterly opposed. Hard as it was, I had to stand behind it before journalists and TV and defend it as "a good idea, since the wage negotiation was taking so long." I received calls from all the CEOs, as well as from the head of the Employers' Federation, basically asking if I was out of my mind. The German parliament wanted to launch a formal inquiry. (That, mercifully, never happened.) I could easily shoulder all that. Far more damaging was dealers reporting order cancellations from angry customers and media coverage stopping just short of calling for a national boycott of Ford products. For a few months, our market share did dip, sharply; incentives went up, and tens of thousands of sales were lost for the year. Our carefully built-up momentum was lost, much to the glee of our competitors.

After the fact, Poling had his "analysis," but it was never again discussed. What was evident to me then, like so many times in my career before and since, was that, once again, the bean counter religion, of which Red Poling was the high priest, living as it does in a world of spreadsheets and budget "timing," hopelessly removed from the unquantifiable reactions of the real world, had cost the company millions of dollars in profit.

In 1977, despite the occasional setback, Ford of Germany was highly profitable and had acquired good chunks of market share from rivals like Opel, VW, and the French imports. These results were sufficient to get me promoted to vice president, Truck Operations, in Ford of Europe. It was an area of the vehicle business I had heretofore known or cared little about, but I soon learned to love it. Unlike the passenger car sector, where brand image drives most of the purchasing consideration, the medium and heavy (Classes 5, 6, 7, and 8 to the knowledgeable) truck business is ruled by logic and cost of ownership. Payload, towing capacity, fuel consumption, and maintenance are what matter in this world: trucks *work,* and the lower the all-in cost per mile, the better.

The European medium-to-light-truck world was rapidly transitioning to diesels, and Ford of Europe, to its credit, was among the first to offer a neatly spec'd four-cylinder diesel in a small, inexpensive truck we called the A-Series. It was ideally suited for farmers, light construction work, and city delivery tasks. With the fuel economy of the diesel, we were able to offer a highly competitive cost per mile, and sales were extremely brisk, outstripping our limited York diesel production capacity.

But all was not well in York diesel land. Soon we heard of the low-mileage failures: broken rods, broken crankshafts, and, most common, a seemingly inexplicable increase in crankcase pressure which ultimately resulted in the dipstick being shot from the engine, in some cases penetrating the hood, followed by a torrential gusher of hot engine oil. Failed engines were at an unacceptable percentage of vehicles delivered, and all occurred at relatively low mileages in an engine category supposedly good for 200,000 miles. Most failed outside the unacceptably short warranty period of time which, if memory serves, was six months or twelve thousand miles. Thus, the owners were stuck with the repair.

We collected and analyzed the mounting stack of returned broken engines and did a thorough root-cause analysis of the failures. Contrary to my early expectations, the failures were not due to sloppy manufacturing or substandard materials: they were due to fundamental shortcuts in engineering which could only be resolved by a major redesign involving, in many areas, higher cost. I went to see Red Poling, now serving as president of Ford of Europe under the chairmanship of a tiny, cherubic Scottish American by the name of Jack McDougall, whose background was in manufacturing.

My plan for fixing the York engine's many flaws, at an investment of, I believe, $40 million, plus a piece-cost increase of $79 per engine, found zero support with my immediate supervisor, Red Poling.

"Why would we want to spend the money?" he asked.

"Because we have a terrible low-mileage failure rate."

"What's the warranty cost?"

"Low. They're failing just out of warranty."

"Then why fix it? Are we sold out?"

"Yes, for the time being, we're sold out, but it's only a matter of time before the word gets out and demand will drop to nothing."

"That's your opinion," said Red, "and I don't buy it.

We're sold out and have low warranty cost. Why spend a fortune in investment *and* increase the cost? I'm not signing off!"

Well, the word did get out, and sales tanked. The issue came to a head during a period of prolonged stateside absence by Red, leaving wee Jack McDougall with the meetings normally handled by Poling.

"This York engine thing is a disaster!" said Jack. "I want to see a plan to get it fixed." By chance, we had one ready, presented it, but did inform Jack that Red had seen and rejected it. "Well, you can't run this business just by numbers. We have to take care of the customers. I hate to spend investment dollars on remedial stuff as much as anyone else, but we have to have a robust, reliable engine. Try to shave the numbers a bit (nothing ever got approved at Ford without that homily), and get it done ASAP! I'll handle Red when he gets back."

Despite all due haste, it took the better part of a year to get the York diesel to the desired level of perfection. It served well for many years but almost always in the small "transit" panel vans. The A-Series truck, the original, exclusive recipient of the early Yorks, prone as they were to spontaneous disassembly, had become salesproof. Every potential single owner or fleet buyer had heard the stories, and this was long before Al Gore's invention of the Internet. It was another negative triumph for the no-nonsense, just-show-me-the-numbers bean counter approach.

In 1979, with the retirement of Jack McDougall, Red became chairman of Ford of Europe and, against the advice of my boss, I was named president. Now it really got interesting. I got to sit at Red's left elbow for hours each day, sitting through endless meetings, textbook examples of obsessive micromanagement.

At head-count budget time (Ford of Europe at the time had about 25,000 salaried personnel, and the number constantly wanted to creep towards 30,000), each of the major functions presented its manpower needs, department by department, section by section, head by head. Some of the VPs arrived with their controllers, bearing up to seven Samsonite suitcases full of backup books. Red listened to all the compelling stories and then typically said, "I won't let you have six. Make do with two. What's next?" The absence of devastation on the presenters' faces soon told me the truth: they were all asking for way more than they needed, knowing their "ask" would be "axed" by half or two-thirds.

It was incredibly time consuming and unproductive. And the rise in head count, which had threatened to reach 28,000 if all requests had been granted, settled in at just over 26,000. Red considered it a triumph of tough, uncompromising leadership. I considered it a con job.

A couple of years later when I (again against his advice to senior management) replaced Red as chairman and CEO of Ford of Europe, I conducted the same budget review. I took one hour at the most. With all the heads of functions in the conference room, I got agreement from all that head count would not go up. "Live with what you have. Reorganize, reallocate, do whatever you want. You just can't add." In exchange, I permitted the VPs to replace attrition without prior approval. This may sound obvious, but under Red's rule, nobody had the right to replace people who had retired, died, quit, or been fired without a laborious, much-detested application to, and approval from, the "Manpower Committee." Abolishing this piece of corporate stupidity more than compensated for my rigidity on head count.

Red Poling was nothing if not thorough. He worked days, often weekends, and far into the night. He read everything that came across his desk if it was corporate. Once, he caught me reading *Auto Motor und Sport,* Germany's leading car magazine, in my office. "If you're doing your job, you won't have time to read car magazines," he said. "Red, I'll *always* make time for car magazines. I need to see what's hot, what's not, and what competitors are doing." "Nonsense. All people want is a car that starts every morning and gets them to work on time. You don't have to read car magazines to figure that one out." Words obviously failed me.

One of Ford of Europe's most time-consuming monthly meetings, presided over by Red Poling, was that of the Project Appropriation and Approval Committee. It was the purpose of this meeting to monitor and approve even the tiniest bits of spending in Ford of Europe's $8 billion empire. There were always hundreds of projects, and the meeting easily consumed an entire working day. The projects costing several hundred million usually sailed right through: they had been squeezed, monitored, and combed through by corporate staffs from their inception. It was the small stuff that got all the attention.

There was the new office chair for the Antwerp assembly plant manager: rejected, resubmit. "Why does a plant manager need a chair? He should be out on the plant floor, supervising. I need an estimate of time spent in the chair as

well as reasons an equivalent chair can't be found somewhere in the operation." The "office chair" was submitted
three times, was rejected three times, and was finally withdrawn. Red used this as an important lesson to me: "If you
fight stuff like this hard enough, they drop it, and we save
money."

Another major battle was waged over the Ford of Germany service rep's replacement Polaroid camera (remember those?), which had been stolen.

Red: "Why does he need a Polaroid camera?"

Answer: So they can take pictures of failed parts to show
to engineering without having to ship bulky parts back to
Cologne.

"How many cameras are out there?"

Twelve.

"Why can't they share?"

Because they are all working in different districts.

"How do we account for the film?"

Say what?

"How do we keep track of the film?"

Stunned silence. Then: What do you mean, Red?

"Pretty simple. If we buy a pack of twelve pictures, how
do we know that failed parts were photographed with all of
them? How do we know he isn't taking the camera home
on weekends and taking family pictures on company film?
Tell you what: you resubmit this next month and show me
a legitimate procedure to monitor and catch unauthorized
film use, and I may approve this."

Needless to say, such a procedure was created, approved, never put into effect, and soon forgotten.

Then there was the parking lot of the Dagenham plant in the UK. One of the many lots had crumbled with age, was causing vehicle damage, and needed $50,000 of re-asphalting. "What are the other parking lots like? How come only this one? What's the downside if we don't do it? If we approve this one, will all the others want new asphalt, too? Tell you what: next month, I want whoever is responsible for the Dagenham parking lots to come in and give me a complete status report, with aerial photos if you've got them. I'm not signing off piecemeal. I need to understand the whole picture."

Next month, when the Dagenham parking lot item came up, a small, timid-looking man in his late fifties got up, bearing an easel and many charts under his arm. He wore a white shirt, a greasy tie, and an aged blue pinstripe suit. Fresh from the last of what looked like hundreds of pressings. Clearly, he was a man of modest station, and this was his big moment. He had no doubt told wife and friends that he, personally, would make the parking lot presentation to Chairman Poling and President Lutz. An easel with charts was put in place in front of the two of us, sitting at the bend of the huge U-shaped table. The pointer shook in the nervous presenter's hand. This moment could be his career highlight or his downfall. Two charts into the world's most boring presentation, the hugely overworked Poling fell asleep. (It was not uncommon: he wasn't getting enough rest. I slept a lot, too, but not due to insufficient nighttime slumber. I routinely dozed off from sheer boredom.)

The presenter stared down at Red's sleeping form in

disbelief. With panic in his eyes, he turned to me. I gave him a reassuring smile and, with a circular motion of my hand, bade him to continue. On and on he droned, going over estimates, plot plans, and photographs, finally arriving at "Conclusions and Recommendations."

"And thus, gentlemen, I conclude my review and hope the information provided has been satisfactory." Poling snoozed on. After a decent interval, I smacked my open palm down hard, startling him into "fully awake" mode, and said, "You are to be commended on an excellent job. You've made your case, and I'm sure the chairman shares my opinion. Isn't that right, Red?" "Yep!" he said. "It's approved." I've always wondered what the little Dagenham parking lot superintendent told his wife that night when she breathlessly inquired, "How did it go, dear? Do tell me all about it!"

One of my major tests as Red's understudy and, hopefully, eventual replacement came during a major Ford of Britain strike. The unions, led by the majority Transport and General Workers' Union, aided and abetted by smaller unions, had withdrawn their labor in search of much higher wages. Britain being on strike was bad enough in terms of revenue and profit effect. Far more ominous was the fact that the now-integrated Ford of Europe, eschewing the old practice of doing everything in every country, now single-sourced many components and shipped them where needed. With the supply of UK-sourced components set to dry up, it would only be a matter of time before Cologne, Antwerp, Valencia, Strasbourg, and all the other plants ground to a halt.

Naturally, Red ordered up elaborate analyses of availability of every critical component, with precise calculations of which continental plant would shut down when. Since he was about to depart on seven weeks of home leave in the United States, he entrusted this vital matter to my semi-inept hands. "You just read it. When do we shut everything down?" he asked.

"I know what those sheets say, Red," I replied. "But knowing how the guys work and what's going on with reactivating German suppliers, and Ford of Britain people smuggling tooling out of the plants and sneaking it to Cologne in the trunks of their cars, I know the continental plants will run weeks beyond what the analysis predicts."

Red was aghast and actually grew angry. "I had our logistics people do that analysis, and they scrutinized everything! Everything! Every tool and equipment status, all inventory, including in transit, matched against continental production schedules. . . . I can give you the exact hour when the plants will run out of parts! A lot of effort went into this, and you blithely reject it! Your problem, and the reason you may *never* replace me, is that you don't trust in data! You think your damn gut is smarter! Tell you what. You write down when you and your gut think the plants on the continent will go down! Go ahead! Do it!"

So, I took the pad he proffered and dutifully wrote, "The continental plants will produce indefinitely, regardless of the length of the UK strike. Signed: Robert A. Lutz."

"Give me that!" Red ordered. "This is going in a locked drawer in my desk. I'm saving it. After those plants go down, I'm showing it to Pete (Don Petersen, then executive vice president of International Operations and Red's boss) to show him why you aren't qualified for higher responsibility."

There was no risk, because I knew that, outside the analysis, the organization was fairly glowing with most unusual entrepreneurial enthusiasm. Many critical tools and fixtures were smuggled out of UK plants and taken to the continent in the trunks of private cars, a practice that Red would never really hear about because it wasn't a company-approved shipping procedure. People were generally afraid to tell him things, but I always thrived on those sources. They gave me a feel for what was occurring in the ranks, and that awareness will provide a better guide to future outcomes than any deep-dive analysis, rife as it is with caution, disclaimers, errors, and safety factors.

I also knew that the Valencia, Spain, plant was rapidly altering production schedules, cancelling Fiestas with the larger UK-built 1.6-liter engine, and substituting lower-end models with the Valencia-built 1.1-liter engine. Throughout the continental plants, schedules were being altered to reflect the probable loss of UK components. It meant less choice for dealers and customers for a while and less option profit in those cases where we could not offer the larger, UK-sourced engine, but production would continue.

With Red safely on home leave, I daily contacted my sources who reliably reported continued progress on, essentially, quarantining the UK strike and depriving the union of its major tactical weapon: the shutdown of all Ford of Europe production. Seven weeks later, Red returned from home leave, knowing that the continental plants had never shut down and that, even if the strike hadn't been settled, they would have produced indefinitely.

I asked Red if I could have my note back. He refused, saying that he was keeping it in his file anyway, because even though I had "lucked out" this time, it served as testimony to my disregard for financial rigor. The theme of my financial recklessness was pressed home repeatedly. During one of his efforts on behalf of my continuing financial education, he once told me, "See, the difference between you and me is that if the devil came to you and said, 'Go $50 over the cost objective on this vehicle program, and I'll make sure it's the best, most successful car ever!' you'd take that deal, and I wouldn't."

"For fifty bucks? You bet I'd take it! When you look at the hundreds, even thousands, we spend on incentives because the car isn't quite what it should be, $50 is a steal!"

Red's face grew . . . red! "And that is why you can't run a business!" he fumed. "Cost targets are sacred, dammit! You start disregarding them, and it's Katie-bar-the-door! [One of his pet expressions.] You lose all discipline! You've *got* to hang your hat on something! [Another favorite.]"

Another disappointment came when Ford's European staple, the Cortina, was suddenly being massively outsold by GM's new Vauxhall Cavalier, especially in the important fleet business. It seems that GM, in a fit of marketing acumen, had provided the Cavalier with a cassette player, high-tech in-car entertainment in those days. The tens of thousands of drivers in the UK's business fleets could choose either a Ford Cortina or the equivalent GM Cavalier from the selective list. The vast majority checked the Cavalier box because of the tape player.

My immediate question to Engineering was, of course, Why couldn't we put the cassette player from the high-end Cortina Ghia into the fleet model? The answer was that the cassette player required speakers in the doors, and we did not have a door trim panel on the fleet models that could accommodate speakers. It was, however, planned for "next fall" and had been designed. Since we were losing many millions per quarter on the stumbling Cortina sales, I asked what it would take to pull the speaker-capable door trim panels ahead, and how soon could we get them. The answer was that if we kicked off immediately, we would have cassette-equipped Cortinas for the fleets by February (this was in October). It would take a couple of hundred thousand in capital, which was covered in the budget, and $70,000 of engineering expense, which was not. So the decision to make was, Do we overrun the engineering budget by $70,000 to protect roughly $12 million of profitability? A no-brainer if I ever heard one. My "accomplice" in this unconventional transaction was one John Kaplan, a brilliant, funny finance guy, one of Red's promising protégés, then controller for Engineering. Jointly, we signed off and congratulated ourselves on having made an intelligent business decision. But Red Poling, when he ultimately found out, was nearly apoplectic. "I'm not surprised you did it, Bob, because you're fiscally irresponsible. But I'm shocked and disappointed with John. I trusted him. I thought he'd go far and was made of the right stuff."

Months later at bonus allocation time, when we laboriously discussed who would get what percentage of their annual salary as incentive compensation, Red's biases came to the fore. The senior marketing people were dismissed with comments like, "He just gets the standard percentage. All he ever does is spend money on marketing!" The finance people, however, were treated like saints and always plused up, except for poor John Kaplan; Red never forgot his treasonous act which struck at the very core of the tenet that budgets are never, ever, *ever* to be overrun, no matter what the reason!

I hated working for Red. It was sort of like Marine boot camp all over again, only this time, I kept asking myself, "Why?" Gradually, unbelievably, the answer began to reveal itself over the months of my suffering. My initial enlightenment came in the formative stages of the second-generation Fiesta, then and now Ford's smallest model, with commensurately small profitability. Product Planning and Engineering presented their proposal: all new, slightly larger, totally wonderful, with a $1.1 billion capital bill. I knew it was more investment than could be justified by the Fiesta's thin margins. And Red, knowing the numbers, said, "Tell 'em they got $400 million; that's all we can afford." In my next meeting with the product development folks, I gave them the bad news. "Your $1.1 billion is now $400 million. Do the best you can!"

The same meeting the following week found the product development folks jubilant: "We're not down to $400 million, which is manifestly not doable, but we're down to $800 million, and the program is still good." I played the Red Poling role: "Come back when you're at $400 million.

Meeting's over." Personally I doubted they could do it, but I was morbidly curious to see what would happen.

The next meeting produced a really, truly, gotta-believe-us rock-bottom number of $590 million. The meeting was over again. I had to steel myself not to cave in, looking at the disappointed, almost disgusted faces of the engineers and product planners. "What the hell has gotten into Lutz? He's acting like Poling!"

Finally, the product development folks came in with the $400 million program—only it wanted to be $450 million. "We can do it for four hundred, but we'd have to carry over the front suspension, which is by far the weakest point of the car and the subject of many complaints. Redoing it would cost $50 million because we'd have to change the engine box, wheelhouse inners, and a lot of hidden stuff to accommodate it. Bob, we beseech you! We have to have that new front suspension to have a credible new car." I was sold and presented it to Red. "Dammit," he said. "You gave in!" They just can't have a new suspension. How many people would notice? Not that many! I don't care what the damn magazines say. They're not our customers. Tell the guys $400 million, and that's it."

The next day, I dutifully passed on the bad news to a shocked and angry head of Product Development. He was quickly gearing up for what I call "malicious obedience." (I'll play your silly game; let's see how you like the piece of crap I'll deliver at the other end, thanks to your skinflint attitude.)

Later in my career, I learned that the "malicious obedience" phase only lasts a few weeks. After that time, the product development guys start realizing that necessity is the mother of invention. "Is there really nothing we can do to that front suspension without spending a ton on related body structure?" or questions of similar content begin to surface. And in almost all cases, as in the second-generation Fiesta, some bright engineer somewhere comes up with a solution. In this case, it involved a clever new linkage, as yet unused by any company, which provided vastly increased suspension travel and basically all of the benefits hoped for in the $50 million "all-new" solution. The price tag was $7 million. I went to Red and said we were getting the new suspension and that the total was now $407 million, and that we should approve it. He agreed, and said, "See? You're learning! That program wanted to be $1.1 billion. We got it to $407 million. The new suspension was going to be $50 million. We're getting it for $7 million. You just have to be an SOB and hold their feet to the fire! Be tough and unrelenting! If they want the product, they'll find a way!"

Well, they won't *always* "find a way," and the leader does need to exercise judgment, but that second-generation Fiesta program, which went on to be a phenomenal success in both volume and profitability, marked an important turning point in how I approached the business. Red taught me that the tough, uncompromising, unfeeling, almost nasty approach to initial cost and investment estimates could produce meaningful savings. It forced the planners to reexamine how much of the tooling and facilities could get reused, how many parts could be carried over from the past model, how many body styles and versions were really necessary as opposed to nice-to-have. The Poling approach served me well during my later tenure at Chrysler and my last tour at GM, although I was always at pains to leaven it just a bit with humor, engineering, and marketing judgment.

Later in his career at Ford, Red had responsibility for Ford North America, during which time the 1985 Taurus and Sable were launched. Against Red's better judgment, I might add. In fact, he collared me in the hall one day and said, "When the Ford Motor Company goes broke, I hope you realize that it was your fault for talking Phil (Caldwell) and Pete (Don Petersen, then president) into the Taurus program. We just did some market research in New England, and they *hated* it. You know what they really liked? They really liked the Chrysler K-car, and that's what we should have done."

He later became president, and then chairman and CEO. Mellowed by the years, he had become a fine leader, pushed for great products, and delivered great results to the shareholders. When I left to go to Chrysler in 1986, Red was genuinely disappointed and shocked. He had, he said, great plans for me, now that I was beginning to grasp the concept of financial discipline.

He frequently congratulated me on my work at Chrysler and stated he was proud of me, his most reluctant, most difficult protégé. We occasionally met for lunch or dinner, and I considered him a friend and supporter. It pained me to see his gradual physical decline, as he had always worked to stay in shape, and I was saddened by his death. I hated him. I loved him. He was, all in all, a fine leader, and I owe him a lot.

8

LEE IACOCCA

CHAIRMAN AND CEO
CHRYSLER CORPORATION
CEO 1978–1992 • CHAIRMAN 1979–1992

The name is an acronym for

"I Am Chairman Of Chrysler

Corporation, Always."

LEE IACOCCA had been trying to get me to join him at Chrysler for several years when, in 1986, disappointed with what appeared to be a bleak career future at Ford, I became interested, and we began talking in earnest.

A deal was soon struck, and I politely exited Ford, conscious as always in my career of the value of a gracious departure with no hard feelings. I arrived at Chrysler eager to set about my tasks as executive vice president, Trucks (which at that point were almost nonexistent at Chrysler), International Operations (likewise), and Diversified Products (typical of the era, the company's own in-house suppliers and component plants).

In my inaugural meeting in Lee's office, his performance was, in many ways, typical. He was effusive, enthusiastic, expressing his opinions with a firmness that left no doubt in the listener's mind that these were *facts* that could not be questioned.

"You picked a good time to leave Ford, lemme tell ya! Those potato cars (Taurus and Sable) they're coming out with are gonna bomb. We put a couple in a product clinic against our own upcoming Dodge Dynasty and Chrysler Fifth Avenue (elongated versions of the K-car, equally boxy, with "Greek temple" grilles, stand-up hood ornaments, padded vinyl roofs, and every dated styling cliché that was driving American buyers to imports), and we killed 'em. Our average score was 7.5 on a 10-point scale. Theirs was a 5.0. It's gonna be the flop of the century. I hope you didn't have anything to do with it."

I knew the story behind the averages. The new Chrysler products were scored around 7.5 by the vast majority of respondents. In words, that means, "Okay, not awful, but not my first choice, most likely." That kind of score, in the modern world, is the kiss of death, because nobody settles for the second choice unless it is made into a deal you can't refuse through costly rebates. Average incentives of $3,000/car is what it took to move the ugly monsters off the lots. The Taurus, on the other hand, was sharply polarizing. Like the first new Dodge Ram pickup in 1994, it triggered a love/hate dichotomy: half the respondents hated it with a passion and assigned it a score of 1 or 2. The other half was stunned in a positive sense and couldn't believe that a U.S. company was launching a car of such modern, import-like appearance. They overwhelmingly voted 9 and 10. The misleading average, of course, was 5. But in today's highly competitive market, "blending in" with 7.5 doesn't work. It doesn't matter how many 1s and 2s you have: the success of the product comes from the enthusiasts who can't wait to buy it. Thus, Taurus/Sable went on to become America's best-selling car, free of incentives, selling for years at a cadence of over 400,000 annually. Chrysler's Dynasty, Fifth Avenue, and, later, Imperial, despite massive rebates (one of Iacocca's earlier marketing inventions: "Buy a car. Get a check!"), never really broached the 200,000 level.

But in my inaugural meeting, Lee was expounding

upon Ford's colossal error. He was, figuratively, rubbing his hands with glee. I wondered: Should I burst his bubble? Should I tell him the bad news the research portended? Would I alienate my new CEO by giving him a market research education he didn't ask for? Wouldn't it just be wiser to shut up and move on? My failure to do just that was typical of the almost teacher/pupil, father/son, love/hate climate that was to mark our rocky relationship. He clearly didn't like the news, didn't like my smart-ass attitude, and, not having had much practice, didn't like an underling telling him he was wrong. There would be many instances in our relationship when the same situation was repeated, sometimes very unwisely on my part, in meetings. It's strange. I find it hard to comprehend a leader who feels threatened by subordinates who offer an honest opinion, who aren't (dangerous) yes-men, who will steer the boss in the right direction. But one of the little-known aspects about Lee Iacocca is that beneath the commanding stage presence, the brilliant performances on TV, the boldness of his public statements, there was a side that was vulnerable and insecure.

Quite possibly, this stemmed from being born in that locale known as "Humble Origins," in this case, the steel-making Allentown, Pennsylvania. Lee's father and mother were both Italian immigrants. Through hard work and a good sense of entrepreneurism, Nicola Iacocca became the owner of a successful hot dog stand, famous throughout Allentown as "Yacco's Hot Dogs."

What Lido Anthony Iacocca lacked in parental gentility, he more than compensated for in work ethic and intelligence. He graduated from Allentown High School in 1942 and from Lehigh University four years later in 1946, with a degree in industrial engineering. Following a graduation with highest honors, Lee won a fellowship to Princeton University where he concentrated on the curious duo of politics and plastics. Joining Ford soon thereafter, his rise through the ranks was spectacular. In a sea of conforming, cautious, quantitative colleagues, Lee was fast, courageous, opinionated, and mostly right. (He wasn't in Engineering very long: he may have had a degree, but his knowledge of what actually goes inside a car or what it takes to produce one always seemed alarmingly rudimentary.) Lee was a born marketing guy, a huckster, a promoter, a supreme salesman, a man who could have run successfully for almost any political office. His talent knew almost no bounds. While his "car guy" gut feel failed to evolve in the late 1980s and early 1990s (he was convinced that Americans would always love vinyl roofs, Greek-temple grilles, opera windows with little gold stripes, and fake wire wheel covers), he was nearly infallible when those design trends ruled.

So why the insecurity, the worry, and the mild case of "imposter syndrome"? It had much to do with the Ford family and the culture of Iacocca's senior colleagues at Ford. Henry Ford II, grandson of the founder, was born to wealth. He was partially educated in France, spoke the language reasonably well, and was perfectly at ease with the key social, industrial, and political figures in Europe. He wore expensive custom-tailored clothes, but they were often casually rumpled, as if to say, "What does it matter? They're the best money can buy. If they wrinkle, well . . ." His ties were always silk, with small understated patterns, in the European manner. Henry Ford II was immensely powerful, yet the power was never projected deliberately. "HF2," as he was known, would never have used the phrase "Do you know who I *am*?" regardless of the circumstance. He just quietly assumed that people knew.

Mr. Ford moved and spoke gracefully, at medium speed, and was painfully polite, even deferential, with subordinates. His lifestyle was not dissimilar to that of a very old, wealthy European family. In short, Henry Ford II was as close as the United States, with our so-called classless society, will ever get to a genuine aristocrat. Gentle, genteel, urbane, casually expecting the best in wine, food, clothing, and accommodation (but never complaining when things weren't quite up to par), he stood in sharp contrast to Iacocca.

No "to the manor born," no silver spoon, no family history of the same Savile Row tailor in London, no illustrious forebears here. HF2 was the scion of America's most successful industrial dynasty; Lee Iacocca was the son of a heavily accented immigrant Italian hot dog vendor.

Even the clothing showed contrast. Lee's suits tended to be more flamboyant—pronounced plaids with wide lapels; the ties were broad, colorful, and in-your-face. I'm reasonably sure HF2 was not, consciously, a snob. But as later events proved, he was never really comfortable with the brashness, the demeanor, the clothing, the background, and the general lack of couth, of class, that Mr. Ford felt was a prerequisite for the highest position in the Ford Motor Company. I doubt it was a question of performance that triggered Iacocca's sudden firing in 1978. Learning of his termination in Henry Ford's office, Lee asked, "What the hell did I do wrong?" With absolute honesty, Mr. Ford famously replied, "Lee, I just don't like you."

Iacocca was a sensitive person. After what must have been periods of being taunted simply for being Italian, after suffering through hundreds of Italian jokes (remember, all this was before the onset of political correctness), after years of vague discomfort around Henry Ford, he was fired not for *cause,* but for who he *was,* and for his background.

Admittedly speculative, armchair analysis may, in part, explain some of Iacocca's occasional discomfort with me. Like Henry Ford II, I was partly educated in Europe and always wore conservatively patterned, traditionally cut Savile Row suits. Through little credit of my own, I speak German and French fluently, and even my marginal command of Italian was better than Lee's. I noticed a degree of irritation on his part during one of our several business visits to Italy when I conversed in Italian, probably causing him to feel vaguely trumped. After all, *he* was the Italian, not I. I learned to keep my linguistic ability mostly under wraps around him because I could always sense an undercurrent of annoyance.

But in a familiar business environment, he exuded confidence and conviction, and prior to my arrival, his judgment was rarely questioned. This sometimes led to decisions that were not for the timid, such as those in the early 1980s that arose from the stunning success of Chrysler's first-generation minivan. The Windsor, Ontario, assembly plant was running flat-out maximum overtime and was turning out over 200,000 units per year. Yet something told Iacocca (who did actively listen to dealers who were perennially short of minivans) that the potential demand would justify a second plant. And the second plant, ultimately located in St. Louis, Missouri, would produce a long-wheel-base version with an optional V6 engine, commanding higher pricing and profitability. Many cautioned against the huge investment, arguing that the minivan, popular though it was, could not sustain a sales rate consistent with a manufacturing capacity of over 400,000 units per year. Iacocca would have none of the hand-wringing caution: he made the decision to go for it, told the timid to deal with it, and was amply vindicated as global minivan volume, in the early 1990s, topped half a million units per year and formed the foundation for Chrysler's newfound prosperity.

It was similar with the acquisition in 1987 of American Motors Corporation (AMC), the fourth American (albeit French-owned by Renault) auto company, but a pathetically small one with a market share of under 4 percent. But it had two things Lee wanted: the Jeep brand and a soon-to-be announced large sedan designed and engineered by Renault specifically for the U.S. market.

It was typical of European thinking at the time that the red-hot sport utility craze was a temporary fluke, and that American Motors needed successful passenger car products. Meanwhile, Jeep Wranglers and the recently introduced Jeep Cherokee were posting record sales numbers. But the French owners failed to go with the momentum in the market and insisted on squandering vast resources on an all-new front-wheel-drive passenger car roughly the size and shape of Ford's successful Taurus. Lee wanted it, and we would ultimately create a new Chrysler Corporation brand for it. It became, after the acquisition, the Eagle Premier. (Faced with the triple liability of poor quality, lack of brand familiarity, and "barely okay" styling, it flopped in the marketplace and was ultimately scrapped.)

Most of Iacocca's senior management was opposed to the AMC acquisition, including me. Chrysler was not flush with cash; management was already spread thin. But our engineering group was excellent and worked fast. Our plants were humming, our dealers profitable. Why risk this adventure, why upset a perfectly promising future just to buy a moribund auto company that had been less than brilliantly run by its French owners?

Lee turned a deaf ear. He tasted conquest, new challenges, new opportunity, grander scale, positive headlines about bringing AMC back to American ownership. He was, again, not about to heed the call for caution, worked with the investment bankers, helped negotiate the deal, bargained with the French, called the whole thing off when we couldn't agree on terms, and patiently waited for the French, desirous as they were to unload this offshore turkey, to come back, which they ultimately did.

The purchase accomplished, Iacocca drove immediate consolidation: all AMC functions were rapidly folded into their Chrysler counterparts, but with a twist. Instead of pink-slipping all the AMC people, as many CEOs would have done with the acquired executives, he used them to improve the breed. To the astonishment and dismay of many Chrysler executives, it was *they* who were let go, replaced by hard-charging, bright, untraditional AMC people. Iacocca's mandate was that, after 120 days, the total salaried head count of the combined companies be no higher than Chrysler's before the acquisition. An exception was made for the Jeep engineering group, which became the rescuing cavalry for Chrysler's own small, under-resourced truck engineering group. The 120-day goal was accomplished, so with essentially the same corporate fixed cost, Chrysler was now selling almost 300,000 units more, 200,000 of which were high-margin Jeeps. The profit impact was profound and almost immediate.

This rapid digestion of the acquired company was a textbook how-to example, in sharp contrast to BMW's kind-hearted, compassionate, money-losing bumbling after acquiring the British Rover Group. Equally shameful was GM's benign neglect of Saab: twenty years after the acquisition, Saab was still being run quasi-autonomously, with all major functions duplicated, in pathetically small scale and with annual cash injections from Mother GM in the hundreds of millions of dollars. Everyone agreed that "Saab needs to be fixed," but nobody ever gave the unmistakable order to get it done.

That wasn't Lee's style. He got it done. With AMC, Chrysler inherited what was originally destined to be the successor to the compact Cherokee. But it was larger, heavier, and more expensive to build—a program that had been victim to "size, mass, and cost creep." Iacocca had a solution. Reengineer and further "premium-ize" it, make it V8-capable, name it Grand Cherokee, run it as the Cherokee's big brother, and build it in an all-new plant on Jefferson Avenue in Detroit. The old AMC folks were aghast: this had not been the plan!

But the Iacocca plan was executed, and the old Cherokee, with some freshening, continued to sell on value at over 200,000 units per year, while the new Grand Cherokee—powerful, luxurious, and expensive—handily filled the new Jefferson plant, three shifts, at 250,000 per year. It was a smash hit: the world's first medium-sized, high-powered, agile (yet off-road capable) sport utility vehicle. Together with the Wrangler, Chrysler had, in a short time, taken the Jeep brand from 200,000 units per year to half a million. It made Chrysler, for a time, the world's most profitable car company. Renault could have done exactly the same thing, but they didn't see it.

Not all was peaches and cream: as stated earlier, the much-vaunted Eagle brand never gained traction. The big Premier was a resounding flop and cost money. Rounding out the Eagle portfolio was a motley group of rebadged Mitsubishi products, which failed to entice buyers.

And at one point, Lee started chickening out. A few months prior to the launch of the Jefferson Grand Cherokee plant, he became convinced that the Jeep brand and Jeep dealers could not possibly retail the capacity of the new plant. We needed, he said, the power of the Dodge dealers, and thus ordered a thinly disguised Dodge version of the Grand Cherokee. He encountered major resistance, of which I was a prominent part. My team and I were convinced we *would* sell two shifts (nobody dreamed of the ultimate three shifts), and that a transparent, badge-engineered

Dodge version would harm the growing value of the Jeep brand. So Lee pushed and reviewed progress; we stalled and invented delays. It wasn't until Jefferson North (as the plant is called to this day) was manifestly sold out that Iacocca reluctantly gave up on his Dodge version.

It wasn't the first or last time that Iacocca showed an alarming willingness to sacrifice brand integrity, stature, and reputation on the altar of full-capacity utilization. Immediately after the acquisition, he ordered a design review of the whole gamut of Chrysler and Dodge products, and restyled them with the familiar Jeep seven-slot grille and Jeep badges. Our collective, horrified eyes fell upon full-size Dodge Horizon hatchbacks, Dodge Dakota pickups, and others, cosmetically altered to look like Jeeps but possessing none of the traditional highly valued capability characteristics for which Jeep was justifiably famous. Fortunately, they all died on the vine, largely thanks to courageous resistance on the part of Joe Cappy, head of the Jeep brand and keeper of the brand integrity flame, formerly the president of American Motors. He had gone from French management that didn't understand Jeep to an American CEO who apparently didn't get it either! To his credit, Joe prevailed, and the "fake" Jeep programs were cancelled.

The acquisition of tiny Italian sports car maker Lamborghini was another addition to the Chrysler brand portfolio that few of us understood, but in Lee's mind, it was a connection to an Italian luxury brand that could be exploited. We paid next to nothing for the company; they were virtually broke and produced only 300 cars per year.

While Chrysler funded (and happily restyled) the next-generation Lamborghini supercar, the Diablo, Lee had other, more grandiose plans for the brand. Calling me into his office one day, he said, "Look, we didn't buy Lamborghini for $25 million just to fund losses on 300 cars per year. I bought 'em for the brand! I want to see what Chrysler products can be upgraded, and, okay, maybe they're not actually Lamborghinis, but they can have a lot of the cues . . . the leather, the prancing bull logo, the wheels . . . we'll call them 'The Lamborghini Edition.' Get going with Design. I want to look at something soon!!"

I dutifully informed Tom Gale, the VP for Chrysler Design and author of a stellar line of Chrysler, Dodge, and Jeep products in the late 1980s through the mid-'90s, and he was dumbstruck. "That's nuts," he said. And I concurred. But Lee wanted to see a car. Tom and I decided that, if anything, the "Lambo Edition" had to be off of Chrysler's most expensive car: the gaudy, front-wheel drive, vinyl-roofed, opera-windowed Imperial. No sow's ear had ever been farther away from becoming a silk purse! But with a spirit of malicious obedience, Tom and I set out.

We took an Imperial, removed the padded top, ripped off most of the gaudy chrome, lowered it two to three inches, and painted it Lamborghini red. The interior was executed in tan, creamy, buttery-soft (but nowhere capable of passing normal durability tests on the automated twisting-butt machine) leather and matching shorn-wool carpet. The road wheels were stock Lamborghini, gold anodized, with the broadly recognized four-hole pattern, badging proudly proclaiming "Chrysler Imperial Lamborghini Edition," and tiny prancing bulls could be found on front, sides, seats, and steering wheel. Even Tom and I, distasteful as we found the whole exercise, had to admit that, with the ornamentation stripped off, the big wheels, the red paint, it didn't look as ridiculous as we had, sort of, hoped. We were afraid to show it to Lee for fear he'd say, "This is great! We're gonna do it!"

We needn't have worried. Even Lee, upon inspecting the pseudo-Lambo a few weeks later, concluded that the anemic push-rod V6, coupled with the wobbly extended K-car chassis and the front-wheel drive, somehow lacked Lamborghini "cred." The idea was dropped.

But Lee's most delusional and costly effort at somehow wrapping Chrysler in the aura of Italian luxury was his foray into Maserati. Said brand was under the stewardship of Alessandro de Tomaso, an Argentine who had, over the years, designed and produced a number of interesting exotic cars. Iacocca's periodic infatuation with things Italian had known an earlier chapter during his time at Ford. With generous funding from Ford, de Tomaso, under then Ford president Iacocca's benevolent supervision, sold Ford the expensive and partially engineered midengine Ford-V8-powered "De Tomaso Pantera," an imposing car beset with a bevy of major reliability issues. It flopped, and extricating itself from the de Tomaso misadventure cost the Ford Motor Company dearly: Henry Ford II, courtly as he was, never felt at ease with the somewhat shady-looking Alessandro de Tomaso, who, in fact, did come across as a charming con man.

Still on very friendly terms with de Tomaso, Lee, now

CEO of Chrysler and unfettered by Henry's misgivings, decided to forge an even better alliance. The idea the duo hatched was to create a Chrysler K-car-based two-seat sports car. Lee thought he was buying Maserati from de Tomaso; it turned out he was only buying rights to use the name, in conjunction with "Chrysler." The "real" Maserati remained in de Tomaso's hands, only now he had Chrysler money as well.

The two-seater was based on Chrysler's K-car-based LeBaron convertible, a five-seater. To make it different and sportier, about two feet of wheel base was removed, eliminating the rear seat. The sheet metal was different from the LeBaron, but the donor car somehow shone through: with its front-wheel drive and consequently long nose, it did not look at all European. But it had a Maserati grille and steering wheel, the previously described rich, tan Italian leather, and badging which, for legal reasons, combined the venerable Maserati trident with Chrysler's chrome Pentastar. It was a busy badge. The nomenclature stated that this mongrel was called "Chrysler's TC by Maserati." The entire drivetrain was Chrysler, as was the chassis. The assembly, however, was to take place at de Tomaso's decrepit old plant in Turin, Italy.

To say that Lee Iacocca was infatuated with his "TC by Maserati" would be a crass understatement. It was like a cherished child to him. It was the start of something big! There would, after the initial sports car success, be other high-end Chryslers "by Maserati," all bearing the Penta-Trident. He even took the entire Chrysler board of directors to de Tomaso's headquarters in Turin, where all were abundantly wined and dined and showered with gifts.

(Mine was a pair of Maserati loafers, the stitching of which parted company with the leather the second time I wore them. Chrysler Legal decided I didn't have to report the [improper] gift, since it no longer existed.)

The board was wowed; they were allowed to drive one or two prototypes around a little park. Lee was glowing triumphantly, basking in the praise and the board's unanimous resolution that, upon introduction, the car be named "Lido," Lee Iacocca's legal first name. (It never happened; Lee liked "TC by Maserati.")

Reality soon set in. De Tomaso didn't have the human resources to put a decent, reliable car into production. In his impatience to have the car, Iacocca dispatched money and engineers to help out. A new paint system was put in, and Alessandro's plant, which Chrysler didn't own, actually began to look like one.

Finally, to the drumbeat of Chrysler PR hype, the first cars arrived in the United States. Lee took the first one; others went to some of his show business friends, like singer Vic Damone. One was even auctioned off at a charity event for $50,000. Lee was jubilant. But as more cars arrived, the problems mounted. Reliability and fit-and-finish were subpar. The automobile magazine road tests were devastating. Despite a money-losing list price of $29,000, they soon began stacking up alarmingly in dealers' lots.

The head of the Chrysler brand was responsible for the marketing of the TC. He had already spent his budget on dreamy, Italian-themed TV spots, showing the TC speeding through quaint villages, replete with buxom dark-haired women and happily waving peasants.

His name was Joe Campana, and at 600 pounds and 6 feet 4 inches, he was the largest human being I have ever seen. (He occasionally dieted down to 500 pounds, but nobody would notice.) Sitting in front of my desk in a tent-sized, sweat-soaked shirt, he told me he didn't dare tell Lee the TC wasn't moving. So he was going to use his incentive budget to discount the car by $4,000. (This would raise the loss per car to roughly $10,000.)

All was well for a while, and a few hundred TCs moved off dealer lots. Then one day, disaster struck. Lee Iacocca heard from a friend who had paid full sticker price that another friend had gotten $4,000 off! I was called to Lee's office. He was beyond irate. "What the hell is going on? Why the discount? This is the hottest car in America! My friends love theirs. Find out who's doing it, and get back to me." I had no choice but to tell him of poor Joe Campana's conundrum and how he had solved it with incentives. "He wrecked my car with his goddamn incentives. Go fire his ass!" I explained to Lee that I really couldn't; my presidency only covered Engineering, Design, Manufacturing, and Procurement. Marketing and Sales were under my "copresident," the late Ben Bidwell. "Fine, I'll have Bidwell fire him, but I'm telling ya, he's outta here." I did break the news to a crestfallen Joe Campana, who wilted into the smallest 500-pound lump of flesh imaginable. He realized he was being fired for failing to do the impossible and, finally, took it like the man he was. He later opened and operated a Chrysler dealership in Vero Beach, Florida.

The unloved "Chrysler TC by Maserati" soon died a premature death in the marketplace. Again, money had to be spent to get out of the deal. I once asked Gerry Greenwald, then chairman of Chrysler Motors (a subsidiary of Chrysler Corporation, under Lee Iacocca) what the final, total, accumulated financial damage amounted to. Gerry either couldn't or, more than likely, wouldn't tell me. My guesstimate is somewhere north of $500 million.

It was just another Iacocca mistake, this one of heroic proportions. In the big picture of his accomplishments, it hardly counts. We were careful never to clearly identify the write-offs as "Maserati-related," and we never mentioned the car in his presence again. He had suffered enough: his pet program had flopped.

My pet program, however, was called Dodge Viper, and it was looking great. The investment would only be $80 million. With 400 horsepower, it would be the most powerful U.S. car in history. At $50,000 retail, it would be the most expensive American production car ever offered to the public. It had an aluminum V10 engine, a six-speed manual transmission, and its appearance was stunning. To his credit, after agonizing a bit over the fact that "his" was a flop and "Lutz's" looked promising, Lee got behind the Viper 100 percent. And it turned out to be a resounding success in reestablishing Chrysler's dented credibility with every community that mattered: Wall Street, dealers, general media, car magazines, and, equally important, Chrysler's own employees.

A good example of Iacocca's often erratic decision-making process became evident with the 1994 Dodge and Plymouth Neon program, a domestically built compact that was to provide transportation that not only was inexpensive but, more important, would help the company meet the CAFE (corporate average fuel economy) mandates. We knew that proposing a small car was not going to sit well with Lee. . . . Profitability on small cars then, as now, was elusive. Plus, if manufactured in the United States, it would be built with expensive UAW labor, which Lee was determined to avoid.

And so, at multiple meetings, Lee would tell the gang that if we were to build another small car, it would be built in Mexico; no way was he going to let it be produced in the United States. In one instance, I delicately pointed out that, regrettably, it *had* to be built in the United States—otherwise, it wouldn't count for CAFE. (This was before the North American Free Trade Agreement; Mexican-built cars can now be counted.) "Lee," I said, "as distasteful as it is, we need the car to be able to comply with CAFE. And we need to build it in the United States."

"I don't need to do anything," he retorted, raising his voice. "We are not building a damn small car in the United States, period. If we need one, we'll get it out of Mexico; what are they gonna do about it?" I calmly outlined the penalties for deliberate noncompliance with CAFE. "Are you telling me I have no choice? We'll see about that!" He was shouting and waving his lit cigar wildly. "Nobody tells me where I have to build anything. I'll do what the hell I want, and they can throw me in jail!" It was clearly time to drop talk of the Neon and move on to some other subject!

Meanwhile, the product development team was busy defining the program. We knew that, despite Lee's irrational hatred of the car, we would have to build it to meet the law. We also knew it had to be low investment and low cost to provide a chance at profitability, scant though it would be. The leader of the Neon team embraced his challenge with patriotic fervor: the goal would be to create an American compact car of good appearance, good fuel economy, fun to drive, but priced lower than the imports while still showing a profit margin—a really tall order that meant minimizing new investment and reusing what already existed. Thus, the new engine was designed around the equipment in the engine plant, not the other way around.

The Neon had the longest wheel base of any compact car, ever. It wasn't a market-driven choice: it was because all of the body shop equipment in the Belvidere, Illinois, plant was set up for that long wheel base, having previously assembled Chrysler's large cars. The interior of the car was a challenge, too, and the team had to argue, horse-trade, and pull out the "let's win one for the USA" emotional rallying cry to try to get the suppliers to an impossibly low target. The breakthrough came when the winning vendor, JCI, suggested that the target was attainable if we would modify our seating dimensions ever so slightly. If we agreed, JCI would be able to reuse the seat frames and adjustment rails from a previous-generation Honda Civic. We looked, we liked, we bought, and we got to the target cost for the interior. No customer ever knew that under all that upholstery, there resided an old, but perfectly good, Honda seat.

We finally had a Neon program that penciled, as the bean counters say, and we were badly in need of approval to be able to make the timing. Iacocca wouldn't hear of it. Finally, the Small Car Platform Team leader had a brilliant idea. He would modify a presentation he had used for his own team and for suppliers. It described the Neon program and its goals, but with a twist: it was a call to arms to regain America's industrial competitiveness, to dump the traditional, expensive ways, to forge new relationships. It worked with all audiences. I told Lee he really should grant the team leader twenty minutes to review his excellent presentation on America's competiveness and, by the way, the Neon. He grudgingly accepted but warned me that "we'd better not be trying to sell that program."

The team leader amped up the presentation. He was born and raised in an area of northern Michigan that once thrived on iron mines, the ore from which was then transported out on Great Lakes freighters. The slide show demonstrated how this once-prosperous region went into decline—mines shut down, schools and churches empty and abandoned, desolate main streets in near–ghost towns with shuttered shops and crumbling wood and masonry everywhere.

"We failed to compete. We failed to fight back. We failed to get competitive," the Platform leader intoned. "Is this what we want for America's last, great industry, the car business? Cede it to imports? Lose all the jobs? We of the small car team say, 'Not if we can help it.' We're fighting back!" And he went on for another twenty minutes explaining how. He ended with an emotional close, emphasizing the historic crossroads at which Iacocca now stood, and how he, single-handedly, had the opportunity to change the fate of Chrysler and American industry.

When the lights came back on, I saw Iacocca wipe a tear from his eye. The scenes of postindustrial desolation and human hardship had touched him deeply. He turned to the small group and said, "Okay, we're gonna do the car. We're gonna show the Japs that we're not down for the count by a long shot. This thing is gonna surprise everybody; we'll knock their socks off! How fast can we get it?"

The blatant but sincere patriotic appeal had transformed a recalcitrant, stubborn opponent into a pro-Neon evangelist. It demonstrated that, like most brilliant salesmen, Iacocca was vulnerable to a good sales pitch. It also showed, in the best possible light, the caring, human side that was so much a part of his nature. The Neon was launched in the autumn of 1993 and was an instant success, selling over 350,000 units per year. It was even profitable, for a while. That's about as good as it ever gets with small cars.

Lee Iacocca was at his finest when energized, when there was a crisis, when he had a sense of mission. I kept notes from one executive committee meeting where he, in an unbroken torrent of clear direction, laid out the course of the company for the next few months.

It went like this: "Okay, so we're bleeding and we can't keep up the incentive spending. Do we give up some market share? If so, how much? We can't give up a lot, because we have to keep the finance company in business. Finance has to figure out the optimal point where we maximize profits. I gotta tell ya, we need urgency here. I hear people say, 'We'll be okay when the LH cars [future large sedans that were launched in 1992] get here.' That's like waiting for the senior prom. Let's see what we can do with the old cars. Let's add value. Can we add standard air bags? Free antilock brakes? Can we be the safety leader and advertise the hell out of it? Lutz, see how fast we could incorporate the stuff as standard. Meanwhile, Gerry [Greenwald], institute a hard salary freeze. Nobody gets hired. Nobody. Quits and attrition don't get replaced. As for suppliers, accelerate the cost reduction program. We need the 5 percent price reduction; they'll give it to us to keep the business. As for the big cars [Dynasty, Fifth Avenue, Imperial], we need a total marketing program. Okay, they're old. But they're great value; they have a lot of standard stuff. Besides, a lot of people *like* that styling. The way we're heading, we won't sell 50,000 units. That's not acceptable. I want to see a plan."

And he went on from there.

"Longer term, we've got to look at teaming up with somebody. This game's getting too rough. Somewhere between Volvo, Renault, Fiat, more exports to Europe, there's a strategic answer. We gotta stop screwing around and find it. We gotta decide what we want out of a tie-up and what we'll give up. So, what do we do if the stock keeps going down? Can it go below $10? Below $6? It could happen! If we had cash, we'd buy our own stock back. Or we'll up the stock options to the officers; we'll all get plenty of booty when the stock goes back up. Remind me to talk to the board.

"But look, this is an emergency. Pull out all the stops. We've got to sell every minivan and every Jeep, every big car, and we have to get the LH on time. I don't like our first-half financial projection, it's close to zero. I'm upping it to $500 million! Why? Because that's what I think we should do, and we'll get there. I hope all this is clear, because I've got it all written on my list with names behind each of them. Any questions? Everybody get out of here, get busy!"

You couldn't help but admire his focus, the ease with which he rattled off every problem and initiative in front of the company. His energy, optimism, and enthusiasm were infectious: he was able, by the power of his personality and his debating skill, to make one believe things that were manifestly impossible or untrue. It wasn't until later, in the quiet of your own office, you'd tell yourself, "Now wait a minute: what I just heard doesn't add up."

I was not to be Iacocca's successor. Many on the board thought I should be, but Lee fought it vehemently. I was too ambitious, volatile, unpredictable, undiplomatic, emotional, and way too prone to saying the wrong thing at the wrong time. In short, I was way too similar to Iacocca! He instituted what he called his "ABL" succession program, and it stood for "Anybody but Lutz." Candidate after candidate surfaced, until, finally, Lee found Bob Eaton, the head of GM Europe, an entity that was hugely profitable at the time. Bob was experienced, polished, polite, well-spoken, and knew the business. He was soon anointed. Before the announcement, Lee gave me his version of the Henry Ford II "I just don't like you" talk. I was disappointed but at peace. My lack of deference, my willingness to engage the boss with an attitude bordering on smart-ass, were coming back to roost. I was to have a great eight years as president and CEO under Bob Eaton's chairmanship.

Lee didn't want to leave; he wanted to be CEO forever. The board, at last, decided it was time for a change. Mercurial, inconsistent, controversial, a little insecure, given to posturing and bluster, Iacocca nevertheless was the incarnation of the successful leader. Blunt and fearless in his public pronouncements (often to the shock and horror of the PR folks, who would have to put out a release saying, "What Mr. Iacocca meant to say is . . . "), he addressed major issues facing the country: our lack of any focus on industry and manufacturing, our blithe ignorance of the damage being done to American industry by the weak yen, which made Japanese cars so much more competitively priced. Wrongheaded opinions or regulatory proposals saw him swing into action, with op-ed pieces or TV appearances. His was even one of the best-known faces on TV, and the public loved and admired him, saw him as the man who saved Chrysler against incredible odds.

Iacocca did what leaders are supposed to do: pursue a bold strategy and inspire subordinates, dealers, suppliers, and shareholders with the power of his spoken word. He made mistakes, acknowledged them, and moved on. He didn't mind being unfair or being accused of not listening enough. So what? The job got done!

He has been called "the greatest American industrial CEO of all time." I'm not one to argue!

9

ROBERT J. "BOB" EATON

CHAIRMAN AND CEO
CHRYSLER CORPORATION
1993–1998

What you saw wasn't

what you got.

BOB EATON was a self-described Kansas farm boy (although he was born in Colorado in 1940) and, like many kids with agricultural experience, he had learned his intuitive mechanical and engineering skills by setting up, operating, adjusting, and repairing farm equipment.

He graduated from the University of Kansas in 1963 with a bachelor of science degree in mechanical engineering. Upon graduation, Bob joined GM and skillfully worked his way up the ranks of the company's then enormous engineering organization. In 1973, he was named chief engineer for GM's so-called X-Body cars, a line of transverse-engine, front-wheel-drive cars which, like the future products of GM's competitors, had to be created with haste and large amounts of capital: looming fuel economy regulations had sealed the fate of America's popular, large, rear-wheel-drive V8 cars, and they needed to be replaced by smaller, lightweight cars which were much more European in format and mechanical layout. It was a huge task, as the X-Body cars were to encompass unique vehicles for Chevrolet, Pontiac, Oldsmobile, and Buick. The size of the engineering task was nearly overwhelming, for not only were the cars new, but they also necessitated all-new engines, transmissions, brakes, and most other systems that comprise a modern automobile.

They were launched on time and to great fanfare and were generally well received. But the enormity of the engineering challenge and the short time to production placed too great a strain on the combined resources of GM and its suppliers. The X-Body cars soon developed a reputation for questionable reliability. The brakes were an area of particular concern with issues spanning uneven braking to premature wear. The federal government soon launched a probe and aimed to prove that, far from being beset by the occasional material and assembly problem, the basic engineering of the braking system was flawed and presented a public safety hazard.

Such a finding would have proved devastating for the company: not only would it be prone to hundreds of millions in product liability lawsuits, but it would have been forced to reengineer the entire braking system and, through recalls, replace the existing systems on hundreds of thousands of cars already in the hands of the public.

The challenge of proving to the media, the government, and the public that the X-Body brakes were fundamentally sound fell on the shoulders of Bob Eaton and presented him with his finest hour. Whether congressional testimony, filmed demonstrations, or televised presentations, Bob handled them all. He even went so far as to publicly conduct some of the trickiest and arguably most dangerous tests personally, thereby showing his personal confidence in the system he had engineered. His intimate knowledge of details, coupled with his natural charm and no-nonsense, just-the-facts manner earned him credibility and respect inside and outside GM, and the effort was crowned a success: all parties (some reluctantly) concluded that the X-Body brakes, although not without problems, were fundamentally sound, properly engineered, and presented no public hazard. The senior GM hierarchy took due note of young Eaton's communication ability and courage in the face of adversity (both key leadership traits), and his career was assured from that day forward.

In 1982, he was named GM vice president of Advanced Engineering and successfully ran GM's then-vast research and development activities in Warren, Michigan. In 1988, Bob Eaton broke into the ranks of senior management, being entrusted with the title and responsibilities of GM Europe, a post he was to occupy until his departure to lead Chrysler in 1992.

GM Europe was not only highly successful at the time but was generating unheard-of profitability. One might well argue that the operation benefitted from the tailwind of a booming European economy and also from a highly successful product line that, given lead times in the automotive business, was largely the work of Eaton's predecessor, Jack Smith.

Meanwhile, at Chrysler, Lee Iacocca, already well past normal retirement age, was under increasing pressure from the board to find a suitable replacement. As president and the father (with a lot of help from an inspired team) of Chrysler's hugely successful new products, I was a logical candidate. But for reasons enumerated in the preceding chapter, I had the dubious distinction of being the subject of Iacocca's ABL (Anybody but Lutz) program. Many names were floated, and many candidates were interviewed. Some were industry luminaries, like the legendary Roger Penske, entrepreneur, former race-car driver, megadealer, and owner of numerous industrial enterprises. He wasn't interested. The name of William "Bill" Hoglund, then an executive vice president at GM, was also mentioned, as was Iacocca's former number two man, Gerry Greenwald, who had left the company a few years earlier to assume the CEO position at United Airlines. Internal candidates included Jerry York, later the chief financial officer of IBM, as well as Chrysler vice chairman Steve Miller, later to gain fame as a turnaround CEO of troubled Chapter 11 companies. I was interviewed by the Chrysler board as well, but it was merely a courtesy. None of the candidates, for one reason or another, passed muster. The situation was getting fairly desperate: the board wanted Iacocca to leave, and he had no replacement.

Then the fickle finger of fate came to Lee's rescue. Deep within the Chrysler Finance Department resided one Fred Hubacker, a kind executive who was partly handicapped by what I would assume was a case of childhood polio. Fred and his wife had been close friends of the Eatons for many years, the wives having both been teachers at the same school. It occurred to Fred that he just might be able to boost his close friend into the top spot at Chrysler, and after checking with Bob Eaton, he duly bounced it off Lee Iacocca, who recognized a golden opportunity when he saw one. A highly placed GM executive! Well liked! An engineer with leadership credentials in charge of an operation that had just reported a $2 billion profit! And to make it even better, he was not one of the rival internal candidates!

Interviews and meetings with the board were soon set up, and Bob Eaton, showing his mature, calm confidence and self-assured manner, which had been honed in decades of facing upward and looking good at GM, emerged as the perfect candidate who met all the requirements while at the same time, of course, not being Bob Lutz.

Bob Eaton was hired, and I was advised that my continued presence in the number two spot would be appreciated. A big disappointment, but in retrospect, it all worked out for everyone.

I made it a point to spend time with my fellow "Bob" as soon after his appointment as possible. I found myself liking what I saw: he was of medium height, only a few pounds too many (slim by contemporary American standards), and well dressed, even if his suits frequently had the professional engineer's signature slightly rumpled look. Bob's features were highly appropriate: handsome, good hair, intelligent-looking, often wearing a confident smile. It never occurred to me at that time, but years later, during a visit to a late-hours nightclub as guests of Mitsubishi, where we all had traditionally clad, highly attentive Japanese waitresses, the reason for my "Where have I met this person before" feeling about Bob Eaton became clear. The waitresses looked at Bob and began to ooh and aah, and titter behind raised hands. I asked what that was all about, and one of the starstruck girls told me, "He look just like Glenn Ford" (noted Hollywood actor of the 1940s and '50s).

There was, of course, the mandatory period of overlap with Iacocca while Bob learned from the master, but after a few months of indoctrination and familiarization, the Ia-cocca era—reign, really—came to a climactic conclusion at a CEO good-bye party that, in terms of size, pomp, and celebrity count, still has to be a world benchmark. This apotheosis of Iacocca's career occurred in Las Vegas, where an arena was rented for the occasion and filled with dealers, suppliers, media, and friends. A huge spiral-shaped ascending platform had been built where the basketball court would normally be. An aging Frank Sinatra, forgetting the lines of "My Way," came close to walking off the edge.

Bob and I, with Iacocca safely in retirement, forged a close team. I had warned him that, while he may have been Iacocca's preferred candidate, Lee's real desire would have been to do the job himself, until death do us part. Bob had seen enough of Lee's Machiavellian side to believe my theory. If he and I were to clash, or fail to form a harmonious team, Lee would have gone to the board and said, "Look, we made a mistake. Eaton's too weak, and Lutz is pushing him around. We either get rid of Lutz, which isn't a good idea given his experience, or we've got to find a stronger CEO. In the meantime, I'm afraid the board has no choice but to put me back in as CEO, only until we can find a stronger guy."

And so, Bob and I agreed that we would work together, mutually support each other in word and deed, and that the last thing either of us wanted was to create a pretext for the imperial Iacocca's urgent return.

All in all, we had a good sharing of responsibilities. As COO, I had, at the next level, a brilliant team composed of VP of Design Tom Gale, executive VP of Engineering

François Castaing, executive VP of Manufacturing Dennis Pawley (formerly of GM and, later, Mazda), executive VP of Procurement and Supply Tom Stallkamp, and Jim Holden, who headed Sales and Marketing. It was a smooth, tightly run team, with lots of informal discussion time during lunch and other meetings. We were fast, because the leadership group was in constant contact with each other; we had a commonality of goals, similar views on what worked and what didn't, and a shared dim view of the myriad corporate obstacles that inevitably impeded progress. Still, agreement on direction was always swift and occurred in about one-fifth the time it would have taken at GM.

Bob observed the team in action and realized it had taken years to create it and hone it to its current performance level. And the proof was evident to Bob, seeing the new products waiting in the wings, all arguably the best, most attractive, and most competitive cars and trucks ever fielded by an American car company.

Bob's considerable intelligence told him to leave well enough alone and not try to insert himself or his authority into something he realized he could hardly improve. And so my "Gang of Five" continued as before, with little or no interference from the CEO, whom I carefully briefed on a regular basis, telling him in considerable detail what the team had decided, and why.

It was, all in all, a good relationship. The products, as they successively rolled out, were hits, and we all made sure that Bob Eaton got most of the credit. Profitability and cash flow were at levels not seen before, and all worries about

Iacocca coming back were banished from our brains. We did agree to let free cash pile up and strengthen the balance sheet, always a vulnerability for car companies in a steep downturn, when cash can bleed out at billions of dollars per quarter. (In 2008, GM went into the steep decline with roughly $15 billion of cash. It was gone in four quarters. Ford had a pile of over $30 billion; they bled as fast as GM, but had greater reserves.)

This emphasis on creating a reserve of cash is always a controversial issue: Iacocca never really let cash build; if it did, he would want to buy another car company, airplane company, finance company, rental car company, or airline! For the risk-oriented, letting free cash accumulate on the balance sheet is almost the equivalent of dereliction of duty. A really smart management team, it is held, would find a way to put that money to use. At the very least, the more daring would say use it to buy back your own stock to raise the earnings per share. My personal experience is that just when companies buy back their own shares, economic disaster strikes, and everybody wishes they still had the cash. Bob and I were of the same mind: set a pile aside for the inevitable rainy day.

But Las Vegas–based financier, takeover king, and MGM casino billionaire Kirk Kerkorian (still a Chrysler shareholder) found our cash pile, which I recall was at around $7 billion (large in those days), an absolutely irresistible target. Using our own cash and a little bit of outside bank lending, he could easily take over the whole company. Using former Chrysler CFO Jerry York as his point man, he launched his offensive.

Bob Eaton, never having been in legal, finance, treasury, or anything nonoperational (much like me, but this was a mess the CEO had to deal with), was dumbstruck. But the requisite small army of bankers, financial advisors, and antitakeover legal specialists were soon in place, and Eaton's responses, public and private, were carefully discussed and orchestrated. It was a tough time for Bob: he felt (justifiably) betrayed by Kerkorian, whom he had seen as a supportive shareholder. Bob wanted the whole thing to go away and was in favor of a quick resolution, one much too favorable for Kerkorian. Our team of advisors did an admirable job in largely blocking bank financing for the Kerkorian takeover bid. Basically, the banks had more faith in the Eaton-Lutz duo than in the "shadow cabinet" proposed by Kerkorian, featuring, as you might suspect, an overly willing Lee Iacocca as CEO.

In the end, we achieved a compromise, bought back a couple of billion dollars' worth of shares, and Kerkorian and York went away (only to resurface in 2006 in an equally ill-fated attempt at a takeover of GM).

The media coverage for Bob Eaton was excellent: he emerged as the mature, steadfast, nerves-of-steel executive who faced down the billionaire bully and his cohorts from Las Vegas and preserved not only his job but most likely the future of the Chrysler Corporation. His former colleagues at GM were amazed. Several, including one who at the time of Eaton's move to Chrysler said the move "improved the quality of both organizations," commented to me that, while they all knew Eaton as a competent executive, they had never seen in him the grandeur, the courage, the negotiating mastery that had resulted in the defeat of Kerkorian. I kept the fiction alive.

Little did anyone suspect that behind the bravura performance was a nice man, inexperienced in all this, with no knowledge of applicable laws or even familiarity with the legal and financial vocabulary of the takeover. It was a case of the leader, out of his depth, being led. As in his tacit acquiescence of my leadership of operations, his instinct told him it was a time to set pride aside and let the better brains find the solution. A firmer leader, eager to put his own thumbprint on the solution, might well have taken a different and far less successful path.

Bob was, like many of us, at his worst when he tried to demonstrate superior knowledge in an area of scant familiarity. A case in point: visiting an assembly plant one day, he loudly declared that there was "way too much inventory piled up waiting to be assembled. Next time I come down, I want to see inventory no more than twelve inches high."

Two days later, Dennis Pawley, the no-nonsense head of Manufacturing, came to see me. "Bob, what do you want me to do? That's an old plant, with too few loading docks. The inventory Eaton saw is the lowest 'just-in-time' level we can attain with the number of trucks shuttling in and out of the loading docks. The guys at the plant have quickly drawn up an appropriation request to add more docks, but it will take eight months and $45 million. I think we'd be nuts to spend it, but everybody is scared: he says the inventory goes, or else."

"Let me handle it," I told Dennis. I went to Bob's office and sat down. When I had his attention, I said, "Bob, you know that excess inventory you commented on during your plant visit? Well, you won't be surprised to hear this but, once again, people took it way too literally, so they've prepared a $45 million project to add more loading docks, just to lower the inventory a bit. It's crazy. It just shows how careful you and I need to be when we make suggestions."

"That's unbelievable," said Bob. "I just wanted it looked at. If it can't be done without spending a lot of money, we'll live with the inventory. Boy, people are sure stupid sometimes." This issue and others like it were put to bed with similar techniques. The more cynical would call it manipulation.

The key leadership lesson here is simple. How much more productive would it have been to ask, "Why is that parts inventory so high?" and listen for the answer, rather than declare the imperious "That's too much inventory. I want it reduced." The former provides knowledge and creates trust. The latter creates needless work, confusion, and fear.

Somewhat deprived of day-to-day involvement in operating matters, Bob turned his attention to matters of leadership and cultural change. This all started on a Monday morning in the weekly officers' meeting, which I jokingly referred to as the "meeting of Toms, with selected Bobs." (We had at least seven officers whose first names were Tom.) Taking his turn to speak, Bob announced that one of the problems with Chrysler was a lack of initiative and leadership in the ranks and that we needed a professional leadership training program. I concurred, enthusiastically, and mentioned that there were now several groups of senior retired U.S. Marine Corps officers who were available as consultants to impart to the private sector the ethics, courage, commitment, and pride that has, over centuries, made the underfunded, equipment-deprived USMC the most effective fighting organization in the world.

Bob rejected this out of hand, saying, "The last thing I want for the company is a rigid, top-down, command-and-control military leadership style. Maybe I'm only saying that because I was never in the service, let alone the Marine Corps."

I replied, "Bob, you *are* saying that because you never served, especially not in the Marine Corps." The Marines, in fact, operate on a leadership style which very much empowers even the lowest ranks to "run their own show." Officers frequently consult lower-ranking personnel for advice, for every twenty-two-year-old lieutenant knows, rank aside, that he or she is of less value to the corps than a combat-hardened gunnery sergeant with twenty years' service. The noncommissioned ranks run the Marine Corps; the officers perform "gentlemanly supervision" and are in training for the higher ranks where policy and strategy are determined. The reason it works so well is trust. Trust that those empowered have the right training—mental, spiritual, physical, and professional—that every Marine receives. It results in a common bond, shared values, and set of ethics. You always trust a fellow Marine, because you know you can.

If that model could ever be imprinted on a civilian commercial institution, it would be a world-beater, and morale would be high as well. But Bob Eaton's vision of "military leadership" came, probably, from B science fiction movies, where the general, seeing the alien monster on the TV screen, says, "Sergeant, I want you to take two trucks, twenty men, six howitzers, and (exactly!) fifty rounds of ammo. Circle around behind that thing, and when I give the word, blast the hell out of it. Lieutenant, you take two helicopters, load them with 'hellfire' missiles, and go for the eyes. It's now . . . 17:20; I want everybody in position at 17:32! Any questions?" I'll bet I've seen variations of that scene in fifty movies. Trust me, that is not the way the Marine Corps, or any other military service, runs its business.

But Bob didn't know that, and the company was soon in the grips of a consultancy which, like all the major companies in the 1990s, peddled "cultural change" at every level. As was the fashion back then, enormous amounts of time and energy were spent on elaborate statements of "Missions, Values, and Goals," all separate documents, endlessly discussed, modified, wordsmithed to death, as if anyone would ever bother to actually read a twenty-line "Mission Statement," or a tedious listing of "Values" or "Goals." It was, to be honest, an endless process which, like the gestation period of an elephant, ultimately produced sizeable documents which were little more than restatements of what most of us would call "common sense."

We also had numerous off-site retreats in places like Port Huron, involving role-playing exercises and pointless inanities like Bob Eaton and I donning server uniforms and chef's hats and serving our hundred or so senior subordinates in the food line. It was supposed to demonstrate that, far from being exalted leaders, we were really kind, humble, accessible, and ever eager to serve the needs of the employees. "Customers" were rarely mentioned, by the way.

The whole endless process basically taught that less leadership is better, empowered employees are happier (true, but do they have the skills, training, motivation, and ethics?), and "teams" will solve any and every problem. (Not without a strong team leader, they won't!) Many framed posters began to appear in all the conference rooms, with quaint sayings like "Everyone's Opinion Has Equal Value" (Really? What about the total idiots who are ever-present?), and "There Is No Such Thing as a Bad Idea," another stupid homily which I would have loved to roll up and stuff down the throat of the author. "Leadership" and "Direction" actually became ugly words. They were considered "inappropriate management behavior" in the new world of fear-free industrial democracy, where happy, stress-free, leaderless teams could engage in endless examination of alternatives, patiently listening to each other's half-baked views and moving no closer to any legitimate decision because nobody was in charge.

The whole emotional, touchy-feely group-hug thing came to its climax at another off-site session at an expensive resort, where Bob Eaton, his voice choking with emotion, addressed his troops with tears streaming down his face. The reaction, as they say, was "mixed." Those who were into warmth, emotions, and "feelings" thought it was great. I thought it was simply awful.

But, in fact, the elaborate effort to create a happy, fulfilling, employee-centric, low-performance culture was doomed without any of us knowing it at the time. The grim reaper of the "new culture" manifested himself to me during my visit to the biannual Frankfurt Auto Show. At one of the interminable VIP dinners, this one highlighted by a postdinner speech by Germany's then chancellor, the pompous Helmut Kohl, I was approached by Jürgen Schrempp, the CEO of Daimler-Benz, makers of Mercedes cars and trucks. After he congratulated me effusively on Chrysler's well-accepted product line and spectacular profitability, he bluntly suggested we merge the two companies and create a global powerhouse, spanning all continents and all product categories, from the smallest, cheapest Chryslers to the largest Mercedes luxury sedans and Class 8 diesel trucks. I told him that I was only the number two guy at Chrysler; he needed to talk to Bob Eaton. He scoffed at this and said, "But everybody knows you're the one that calls the shots." Maybe so, but, I explained, mergers are the stuff the "adults" handle: he needed to talk to the CEO.

I reported all this to Bob Eaton upon my return. He was excited because the gathering clouds of Asian competition, coupled with ever more U.S. federal fuel economy and safety regulations, were a source of increasing worry for every Western producer. "Size" and "scale" seemed an attractive counter.

Jürgen Schrempp soon came to Auburn Hills, and he and Bob sketched out the beginnings of what was, in a few months' time, to be heralded as a "merger of equals," uniting two large automotive companies into a powerful combination, to be administered by "co-CEOs" Schrempp and Eaton. Lawyers and investment banks were engaged, the deal was refined, the price per share was agreed upon, both boards blessed it, and the deal was done late in 1998 to huge applause.

I was not to be part of the new company. Aged sixty-six, I had already received a one-year dispensation from the board-imposed sixty-five-and-out age limit, which had been adopted to prevent, rigidly and absolutely, another Iacocca-type personality repeatedly talking the board into yet another contract renewal.

But I suspect there was more to it: both Eaton and Schrempp were well aware of my experience in leadership of German companies, as well as my ability to speak, read, and write German. There may well have been the fear that I could have become the "controlling link" in the merged companies. In actual fact, as things transpired, I believe I could have prevented much of the chaotic misjudgment, misdirection, and mismanagement that would soon characterize the powerful but cumbersome DaimlerChrysler.

Even the name was cumbersome. I remember the pundits in the automotive press joked about coming up with a new name. One tongue-in-cheek bit of speculation was that the Germans suggested they merge the two names, using the "Daim" from Daimler and the "-ler" from Chrysler . . . hence making the new name "Daimler." It was not an inaccurate assessment of how things were to turn out.

Soon after the merger, Jürgen Schrempp moved into my old office on the top floor of the Auburn Hills headquarters building. A tall man, with a powerful, commanding physique and a stentorian voice, a heavy drinker and smoker, always seconded by his lovely secretary, he was, to put it mildly, a brash giant next to Bob Eaton's small, slightly rumpled, slightly pudgy, and generally low-key appearance.

On his first day, Schrempp lit a large Cuban cigar. Bob Eaton quietly pointed out that Chrysler had a general no-smoking policy. Schrempp roared with laughter. "You mean you *had* a no-smoking policy. But, fine. It's in place everywhere except where I want to smoke, which is in my office and the executive conference room!" Bob Eaton said nothing. It was a bad precedent. Soon thereafter, in the executive dining room, Schrempp asked for a good, chilled California white wine. (Consumption of alcohol during lunch is the norm in Germany's executive suites.) "Er, Jürgen, we, ah, don't, umm, serve alcohol in this building," Bob managed to stammer. "The hell you don't! Waitress! Have someone go out and buy six bottles of good, chilled white wine! We're all having some, aren't we, Bob?" Another semipublic humiliation. It was pretty clear that this was *not* going to be a jointly run company, and Bob soon departed, richer by a reported roughly $250 million.

The fortunes of Chrysler soon went south. Losses piled up. Bob Eaton's successive successors, Tom Stallkamp and Jim Holden (both fine executives, but ill-qualified as CEOs of a subsidiary under the autocratic leadership of the mercurial Schrempp), were soon ousted and replaced by an all-German, all-Mercedes executive team who, failing to understand the U.S. Chrysler customers, oversaw a new product portfolio that was largely off target with the notable exception of the big rear-wheel-drive Chrysler 300 and Dodge Charger, basically in place before the German takeover.

The merger ultimately failed, the stock tanked, and Chrysler was sold to Cerberus, a private equity firm, for next to nothing. Their stewardship of the company was even worse than the Germans'.

Bob Eaton became a pariah, the architect of Chrysler's semidemise, the gullible fool who had been tricked by the worldly Jürgen Schrempp, the man who gave away Chrysler but enriched himself. Iacocca, of course, weighed in, stating that choosing Eaton as his successor was the biggest mistake of his career: "I should have picked Lutz." I supposed this last accolade, of sorts, should have pleased me. It didn't.

What got lost in all the vilification of Bob Eaton was that he had done what the private enterprise system expects of its CEOs: he ran a great company, made it a desirable partner, and merged it into a larger company, in the process creating enormous wealth for Chrysler's shareholders. How soon everyone forgot the thanks and the kudos for the "brilliance of the merger."

Bob Eaton had his reputation unfairly tarnished. He was tagged a pathetic loser. By the important metrics on the scorecard, he was a winner.

10

ARTHUR M. HAWKINS

CHAIRMAN AND CEO
EXIDE TECHNOLOGIES
1985–1998

"The Felon"

TO MAKE it clear at the outset: unlike my experience with the other subjects of this book, I never actually worked for Art Hawkins, but I was his successor at what was then the world's largest producer of lead-acid batteries, so I had to deal with his legacy.

My forced acquaintance with Art began after my expedited retirement from Chrysler following the so-called merger with Daimler-Benz. I had spent a few months executing what I had believed to be a sound postretirement plan: some leisure, some interesting board memberships, promotion of my first book, *Guts: The Seven Laws of Business That Made Chrysler the World's Hottest Car Company,* and appearing on the paid lecture circuit. It was not fulfilling. At age sixty-six, I felt that perhaps I was late to mature; I was just beginning to grasp adequately the principles and practice of effective leadership and the complexities and challenges of running a $100 billion car company. Somewhat immodestly, I felt that putting me out to pasture was a waste of a valuable resource.

What a joyous day, then, when I received a call from Dick Bott, at that time a vice chairman of Credit Suisse First Boston. "How would you like to be CEO of a Fortune 500 automotive supplier?" Dick asked. I remember my spontaneous, impulsive reply to this day. "Sure, I'd love it! Whom are we talking about?"

Dick went on to describe Exide, the departure of its senior executive team, the legal issues with various states over allegations of fraud, but, frankly, nothing that sounded too difficult to overcome. My meetings with the Exide board went well, and we quickly came to an agreement over contract duration and compensation. Neither the board, which voluntarily resigned because they had served under the discredited Art Hawkins, nor I had any clear understanding of the intractable mess the Hawkins regime had left behind.

Art had for years ruled the company as if no published laws or statutes, federal or local, applied to Exide. The salespeople were encouraged to resort to bribery to make important, multimillion-dollar battery sales. People joked that Exide made the lightest batteries in the industry because for any given rating marked on the battery, Art had ordered removal of a portion of the lead plates. This reduced weight but, more important, it reduced cost. To the buyer, it meant not getting the battery performance promised by the label. Art didn't like the practice of scrapping returned batteries; many were, in fact, free of defects and returned simply because they didn't fit properly in a certain model. Still, the law is the law, and a used battery cannot be resold as new . . . unless you were Art Hawkins. Under his pressure, returned batteries were cleaned up, relabeled, and resold as new, thus reducing warranty expense and boosting profits. Exide was soon under indictment by the state of Florida, and others followed suit. A major battery sale to Sears, under their famous "DieHard" label, was obtained by bribing the senior Sears battery buyer, who was later imprisoned. Attempting further expansion in Europe, but stopped by European antitrust legislation, Art went to a leading continental battery maker and proposed a scheme of secret collusion and price fixing, which even this firm, operating in an environment more tolerant of industry collaboration than the United States, found offensive.

Mr. Hawkins, then in his fifties, was obsessed with youthful virility (which apparently must have been fading), so he self-medicated with testosterone pills. Most doctors agree that testosterone cannot effectively be administered orally, but that didn't stop Art. According to survivors of his regime, he swallowed quantities of the stuff. Alternating between fits of depression and exuberant vitality, he loudly boasted of his sexual prowess in the presence of female employees, who found it offensive.

Legislation regarding such pesky things as equal opportunity employment and affirmative action were routinely shrugged off as harmful nuisances. The financial results weren't satisfactory either and required constant cosmetic retouching; after all, Art and his senior leadership cohorts owned many shares and held options for many more. Art, poor financial results notwithstanding, was not about to skimp on the imperial lifestyle; this profitless company owned a Canadair Challenger for the exclusive use of Art Hawkins and his family. Valued at $17 million, it was known to make flights to Europe to bring back antique furniture for Art's "cottage" on Mackinac Island, a tony summer resort in northern Michigan. The Exide board, seeing the bad results and the mounting legal challenges, fired Art, his chief operating officer Douglas Pearson, and chief financial officer Alan Gauthier. No one person, not even Art Hawkins, could have committed that much malfeasance without a bit of help!

Shortly after my appointment as Art's successor was announced, I met him at a small birthday party for one of his Mackinac Island friends. Friendly, self-confident, effusive, Art congratulated me on my appointment, and, taking me aside, proceeded to tell me what a thoroughly corrupt organization I would be inheriting. Taking ballpoint to paper napkin, he said, "I'm going to give you a list of who the really bad guys are. If you have any hope of saving the place, you've got to get rid of the guys on this list as soon as possible." The list grew longer and required a second napkin. "Art," I finally asked, "if these guys were so corrupt, why didn't you fire them?" "Are you kidding?" replied Art. "I was so crooked myself that I couldn't lay a glove on them!" This cheerful, uninhibited admission of his own criminal conduct was just one of the stranger sides of Art's troubled personality.

Meanwhile, my entry into Exide as CEO was as weird as Art's behavior. After many meetings and all-employee videos explaining the new, zero-tolerance ethical policies, I had to encourage dozens of experienced salaried employees, all tainted and many on Art's list, to leave the company. I had no president and no chief financial officer for a while. We had to explain to the board that hired me that they were tainted, too, for their failure to probe Art's behavior. We had to replace the accounting firm for the same reason: they hadn't been complicit; they just hadn't done their job.

The Canadair Challenger was sold; this company had

no business owning an expensive executive jet. We instituted mandatory professional ethics training and encouraged the hiring of qualified minorities. The new board included John James, a respected African American businessman who assumed responsibility for ensuring racial and gender diversity.

I personally visited all of our major customers and some former ones. Several of the latter told me that, new regime or not, they would never do business with Exide again. Wal-Mart's reaction was the same. Barely polite, they told me to leave. They would not do business with companies under indictment. Hat in hand, I paid a visit to the Florida attorney general, Bob Butterworth. This worthy individual proceeded to berate me and treat me as one of the criminals. My sense of honor as a former Marine officer was impugned, and I gently brought my military background to General Butterworth's attention. "It doesn't matter," he said. "You corporate guys are all crooks. I've seen hundreds of you in this office, and most of you are guilty." It was not a good meeting, but typical of what we were facing daily in all areas.

Exide was looking at a really intimidating balance sheet. Art, in his acquisition frenzy, had amassed prodigious debt, which in total outweighed shareholders' equity ninefold. Despite a reasonable EBIT (earnings before interest and taxes), the servicing of the enormous debt consumed it all. Logic and the investment banks (Dick Bott and Credit Suisse First Boston in the lead) dictated that we issue more equity and use the cash to pay down debt, so as to halve the interest cost and actually have some EBIT left over for the company's owners. All agreed it was a wise move and even the large shareholders recognized there was currently no EPS (earnings per share) and that a 90 percent debt-to-equity ratio placed the company in a highly overleveraged situation.

All was proceeding according to plan until we announced the plan to the SEC, who immediately advised us that a company under indictment by several states and with such a recent history of criminal mismanagement would definitely not be permitted to issue new equity. This now placed Exide in a checkmate situation. We desperately needed cash to restructure both the balance sheet as well as operations. But we had none; we couldn't go to the equity market, and nobody would sanely recommend more debt. There was no way out.

A few months later, an astonishing opportunity presented itself. GNB, one of Exide's U.S. competitors, was owned by Pacific Dunlop, a very successful Australian conglomerate. In its portfolio, GNB was an underperforming asset and had to go. I saw value in acquiring GNB, in that, while weak in automotive batteries (an area of Exide strength), it had a rapidly growing and hugely profitable presence in the seemingly insatiable market for telecommunications batteries. Exide had no presence in this area, and it was the time of the dot-com boom! An Exide-GNB combination was a compelling proposition; GNB's automotive business could be wound down, thus eliminating its losses, and future supply of GNB batteries by Exide assured full capacity utilization. The projected financial picture for the new, larger Exide was so favorable in terms of profit and cash flow, hence ability to service the even larger debt load, that the scheme drew wide support. The money was found, the deal was blessed by the Justice Department, and it was consummated. I was very pleased with myself, having, through a bold move, saved the company. But the glow of warm self-congratulation soon was displaced by the chill reality of the sudden collapse of the dot-com bubble. With it went the demand for telecommunications centers and their huge arrays of expensive batteries.

What a few months before had been six-month delivery times now turned into a glut of telecom batteries, cancelled orders, slashed prices, overcapacity, and losses. We had bet on a bright future, but the market fell. Chapter 11 was, in the final analysis, the only option. It would have happened without the GNB acquisition, which looked to all like an intelligent risk. A failed Hail Mary. Meanwhile, a jobless Art Hawkins was reported as wandering through rural Michigan in monks' robes, bearded, with hair down to his shoulders, presumably in sandals, the holy Bible tucked away in a pocket or under his arm. A seemingly destinationless pilgrim, aware of the multiple legal proceedings pending, ashamed before the Almighty for his past lavish lifestyle and above-the-law hubris, he may somehow have hoped that God, seeing his object humility, would intervene divinely and make it all all right again.

As it happened, God apparently was not fooled. Brought to trial in the U.S. District Court of Southern Illinois, Art Hawkins, now carefully groomed in an expensive suit, white shirt, and tie, was tried, found guilty, and sentenced to ten years in a federal penitentiary. The conviction was for fraud and racketeering. Interestingly enough, the Exide fraud and executive convictions predated the much larger and more publicized Enron collapse.

Art Hawkins, a leader with ambition his abilities couldn't satisfy, was at least the first of what was, in following years, to be a steady stream of executive imprisonments.

11

G. RICHARD "RICK" WAGONER

CHAIRMAN AND CEO
GENERAL MOTORS
CEO 2000–2009 • CHAIRMAN 2003–2009

Superior intelligence and human

qualities don't always win.

IT'S TOUGH to write about Rick Wagoner, mostly because I like him so much. In contrast to other executives I've known in my career, some covered in this book, Rick Wagoner showed little in the way of "peculiarities." As a leader, he was always polite, kind, and ready to hear opposing views without anger or even visible irritation. His executive suite was modest, as was his style: he eschewed executive trappings and even excessive compensation, believing, correctly, that he was not an imperial ruler but a servant of the shareholders and thus simply a hired hand.

All of this genuine humility, devotion to the company, and self-effacement was improbably packaged into a physical presence that suggested the opposite: Rick stood a square-shouldered six foot five, with no visible fat. A lifelong athlete, he had played freshman basketball at Duke University and earned a degree in economics in 1975. He attended Harvard Business School and received his MBA in 1977.

Rick then joined GM as an analyst in the New York Treasury Office, or NYTO. This operation, far removed from the automobile business as most of us know it, has long been the breeding ground for future GM CEOs. In fact, in the pantheon of former GM CEOs in my memory, only one non–Treasury Office executive was ever able to wrest the brass ring from the eternal clutches of the bean counters, and that was Bob Stempel, an engineer. His tenure ended badly and abruptly, so the selection criteria went right back to "T.O. alumni only . . . others need not apply."

Wagoner's rise was rapid; he headed GM's important Brazilian operation in the mid-1980s. He became GM's youngest chief financial officer in 1992 and president of North American Operations in 1994. In 1998, he assumed chief operating officer responsibility, serving under CEO Jack Smith.

It was during his years teamed with Jack that Rick did some of his finest, yet little-heralded, work. GM at the time was known on Wall Street as a "great destroyer of capital," and it was true. Huge, unwieldy, duplicative in all it did, GM had, over the years, developed a self-perpetuating, self-reinforcing, and self-nourishing bureaucracy that cost more and more and produced less and less.

Jack and Rick realized that the situation was unsustainable. They set about with enormous determination and energy whittling the gluttonous organization down to size. This is not the glamorous part of the car business, the part where one creates new styles, sees them through to production, attends introduction meetings, and speaks before enthusiastic dealers or an interested press. No, the restructuring effort is a dirty, nasty business: eliminating divisions, groups, functions, titles, most held by longtime colleagues and friends. Countless weeks were spent listening to counterproposals, or to why the "other guys" should be shut down, not one's own operation. There were no thanks, no cheering, and little attention from the media. It was just endless drudgery, like hacking through a piece of property covered in underbrush with surgical instruments, trimming away the unwanted weeds while carefully maintaining operational capability. It was like, as one wag once commented, "rewiring a Boeing 747 in flight."

The effort, arduous and long as it was, proved successful. Several engineering groups became one. Fourteen different purchasing organizations were unified, bringing procurement discipline to GM for the first time ever. Organizationally, GM was the equivalent of a 350-pound man who had painfully shed 150 pounds.

Rick's ability to argue, persuade, and persist was instrumental in the relative success of the "back to basics" initiative. It was, perhaps, inevitable, given the extreme focus of the two top executives on the restructuring effort, that the actual "automobile business" part of the corporation was delegated to lower operating levels and did not receive the extent of senior management attention that I have always maintained is necessary for success. GM had, in fact, a recent history of introducing cars that were mediocre, mostly competitive but without a clear-cut purpose or "reason to buy." To me, it was a fairly clear case of an essentially unsupervised organization with no cogent direction that found consensus among the various internal stakeholders and produced vehicles that met the all-important internal targets but failed to resonate with customers.

The lack of true product focus and the damage it can cause had not always been evident to Rick Wagoner. In one interview during the 1990s, when asked why GM had so many finance people in top positions and, apparently, no "product guy," Rick carefully explained that this "product guy thing" was vastly overrated: if you had good designers, good engineers, and good manufacturing people, they would ensure product success. I remember reading that interview and thinking "And symphony orchestras don't need conductors, and professional sports teams can do without coaches." It just doesn't work.

Many product disappointments and outright flops later, Rick, not a "car guy" himself but enormously intelligent, realized that a key element was missing and, to everyone's amazement, hired me as vice chairman for Product Development.

My appointment put lie to the oft-cited "incrementalism" and "caution" attributed to Rick. Those two traits were indeed significant, but Rick was also comfortable with the occasional bold, strategic move, even if it entailed risk. Bringing someone like me on board who was critical, vocal, opinionated, direct, a willing object of media attention, and capable at times of eclipsing less visible bosses was contentious in the GM system, and many of the "lifers" predicted chaos and disaster resulting from my tenure.

Rick Wagoner's support of my efforts to revitalize product development was exemplary, a clear demonstration of one of his most endearing characteristics: steadfast loyalty to his handpicked subordinates, leaving them with the certainty of the boss's backing. Sadly, this otherwise laudable leadership trait can cut in both directions: Rick, in many instances, was devoid of objectivity when it came to people with whom he had served a long time, who had moved up the ranks with him, or whom he had known as early as his

Treasury Office days. It was painful to see Rick protect and support many officers who, to my eyes, personified the large corporation culture of "look good, sound good, prepare well for meetings, and never disagree with the boss." It wasn't until after Rick's departure in 2009 that the hammer fell on many of these experienced, slick, intelligent, but ultimately near-useless members of the Wagoner team. A collective sigh of relief marked their departures.

Rick was definitely a procedural executive. He was blessed with truly exceptional intelligence, mostly left-brain analytical but, unlike in Red Poling, combined with an understanding of right-brain value. Rick liked to reduce complex interlocking issues to understandable, repeatable processes. Given the impenetrable thicket and lack of executive discipline that he inherited, this unquestionably provided clarity and value. The good thing about focusing on process is that it ensures repeatability and predictability. The bad thing about overfocusing on process is that it discourages creativity, experimentation, and new solutions. Yet, in large organizations, many derive comfort from following "the process," even if they know the result will be mediocre at best. Rick, with his well-ordered mind, liked process and was not comfortable in its absence.

On one occasion, eager to show Rick the benefit of free-flowing creativity, I asked Design to put on a presentation of any and all ideas for future vehicles the most talented of the designers could come up with for new, untried ways to put the public on four wheels. It was a great exercise and, as always in acts of spontaneous creation, no "focus groups" had been involved because they could no more have imagined these cars than focus groups of cell phone users could have come up with the iPhone.

We presented it all to Rick, who was fascinated. He just had one question: "How do we know whether these directions we're going in are correct?" I assured him that we would all recognize a potential home run if we saw one, but that these "what if" proposals had to be seen as the products of the fertile imagination of talented designers; they were not firm "product proposals" but rather "thought provokers" or "idea starters." Rick still had a problem. How did we know we were exploring in the right direction? He then outlined his idea: What if we were to create a high-level panel of leading thinkers, artists, architects, fashion designers, people who were young, sharp, cool, and trendy? Expose them to these design "stimuli" in a scientific way, tabulate the results, and we would soon see if we were headed in the right direction.

"Rick," I said, "here we are trying to demonstrate one way to generate new ideas through an unfiltered creative process. But you are so quantitatively data-focused, you immediately want to measure, sift, analyze, and generally left-brain-control what is supposed to be a pure right-brain exercise." Rick laughed and said, "I guess you're right. . . . I always want to see data."

And see data he did. Under Rick's leadership, many quantified "metrics" were established and pursued, the theory being that if we succeeded in achieving every operational goal, success as a car company would be ours. Thus, the company relentlessly pursued "Assembly Hours per Car" (which drove the manufacturing people to move a lot of subassemblies out of the plants to suppliers, at a higher cost) and "Time to Market," a metric that drove some half-baked "solutions," like the Pontiac Aztek, the rapidly developed answer to a question nobody had asked. A compliant team of executives will usually compromise common sense and judgment (both hard to explain) in the interest of "making the objective," for therein lies safety, approval, and possible advancement. We had metrics on "Average Cost per Stamping Die," "Bill of Material Reuse" (percentage of known, trusted parts from the previous model incorporated in the new one), and "Percentage of the Supply Base in New Sources" (a euphemism for countries like China, Taiwan, etc.).

All of these initiatives, and there were dozens, are in and of themselves useful. But too much emphasis on them in the case of personnel evaluations and/or compensation will just about guarantee that the organization will find ways to hit (or even beat) every single metric without any real operational improvement, cost reduction, or improvement in timing having taken place. Of particular concern to me was the lack of focus on product excellence. To be sure, you can create a car with a 90 percent BOM (Bill of Materials Reuse), develop it quickly using low-cost dies with components from "New Sources," and assemble it in eighteen man-hours. But is this a car that will be successful, will wow the customer with styling and features? Or is it just a "numbers car"—a vehicle that met all internal criteria but failed to resonate in the marketplace? In GM's case, it was, with depressing regularity, the latter.

The desire for quantification and order reached, to my mind, bizarre proportions during the annual PMP (Performance Management Process) ritual. Here, every executive, including all the officers of the automotive strategy board, were required to fill out forms containing a large number of next-year objectives, quantified if possible. Given the "matrixed" nature of GM's structure (functions intersecting with geography—the bane of every global organization), all of these goals (most of which transcended the reach and influence of any one executive) had to be matrix-tested. Was global Product Development's set of goals compatible with those of the head of Brazil? Were those of Procurement and Supply compatible with those of Manufacturing in each geographical region?

The task of "box-balancing" (the GM vernacular for the matrix-testing of goals) consumed inordinate amounts of time and internally focused effort. Rick, despite the time and effort spent, saw value: he argued that it would "get people aligned" around goals. I disagreed. The speed with which the outside environment changed rendered all of that massive, staff-supported PMP paperwork useless: profit goals, sales volumes, plant utilization, supplier savings . . . it all became moot the minute the market dropped, as it reliably did these last fifteen years or so. Not being fools, almost everyone saw goal attainment evaporate by about February, and the complex, expensively created PMP goal documents remained safely at the bottom of the desk drawer, never to trouble those of us who could figure out what to do in a dynamic environment again. But the PMP was dear to Rick because it represented stability, predictability, and order in a GM world that was coming apart at the seams.

Another curious "improvement" was the conduct of the monthly ASB (automotive strategy board) meeting. This all-day affair (referred to by one irreverent colleague as "Groundhog Day," after the hit Bill Murray déjà vu film) covered what was at least a thirty-five-item agenda. Although available electronically, it was also present in the form of a massive, tabbed, four-inch-thick binder. In an attempt to speed things up, everyone was expected to read all of the agenda items in advance, comment on them, ask questions if not fully satisfied, and, often, vote approval or disapproval. This resulted in a fairly chaotic set of activities involving many questions on each item (most written by the given officer's staff, and cleverly worded to demonstrate the bottomless curiosity and immense business acumen of the questioner), staff-prepared answers, more questions, and more answers. The last cycle of Q&A was then reviewed in the ASB meeting, with each questioner (always the same ones) being asked if they were satisfied. Inevitably, they were. The ASB meetings still took all day, but now they were devoid of any spontaneity, or any spur-of-the-moment exchange between intelligent, seasoned executives.

Stylistic quibbles and preoccupation with "process" aside, Rick demonstrated many of the qualities of the ideal CEO. He was honest, unflappable, fair, and possessed of a marvelous intelligence. He generally set the right priorities, and often demonstrated considerable courage in pursuing initiatives he felt were important, even if they weren't supported by the rest of his team. The heavy emphasis on China is an example, as was his relentless struggle to reduce the impact of UAW legacy costs without engaging in a destructive strike. The purchase of the moribund Daewoo Company in Korea found little support and yet is now one of the cornerstones of GM's global small car strategy. Rick was persuasive, mentally agile, and an excellent verbal communicator (although his style was matter-of-fact and lacked the populist, emotionally charged oratory of Lee Iacocca).

Rick trusted his direct reports and rarely micromanaged, sometimes to a fault. He was slow to see the weakness or ineffectiveness of some senior executives who looked good, sounded good, and actually did little or were indecisive, but who had come up "through the ranks" with him. In short, he tolerated less-than-stellar performance. Rick was a curious blend of new, young, hand at the tiller, determined to change (often with success) the old, encrusted GM methods yet himself partially a product of that same stable, predictable, plodding culture, tolerant of mediocrity, tolerant of massive amounts of meaningless and unnecessary staff activity.

To the vast majority of his charges, Rick Wagoner was an admired and beloved CEO. His minor faults were easily forgiven, because people felt secure under his leadership. Devoid of bluster, autocracy, and punitive behavior, Rick was the very picture of a leader who genuinely cared about his people. It's an admirable human quality, but it did not serve the company well when the world began to unravel. Rick found it difficult to order tough calls, like downsizing dealers or cutting brands. He talked frequently about the desirability of the latter, yet never imposed his will against resistance, including my own. At some point, if convinced that Pontiac, Saturn, Hummer, and Saab were all "surplus to requirements," a tougher, less caring CEO would have said, "Look, I'm all done arguing. Don't show me any more justification for keeping them. I've seen all that, and I don't believe it. I'll give you ten days, and then I want to see a complete plan for the wind-down or sale of each brand. And don't pad the cost numbers to show me how dumb I am. I just won't believe them. So, get going. Any questions?" Frankly, that's how Iacocca would have done it.

In assessing this first-class human being, especially after his "resignation" in 2009, I'm reminded of one of the main characters in the novel (and motion picture) *The Thin Red Line.* It's the story of a Marine unit during the World War II invasion of a Japanese-held island. One of the main characters is a captain, a company commander and officer, bright, well-trained, disciplined, respected and loved by his men, with that loyalty returned. During the big assault, climbing the steep mountainside from the beach, the company commander's unit is pinned down by murderous Japanese machine-gun fire. Crouching behind large boulders, the captain determines that the hill can't be taken without sacrificing a large number of his troops.

Meanwhile, down on the beach, the battalion commander is screaming into the radio, demanding to know why the assault has bogged down. The good, honest, decent captain can't bring himself to send his men to their deaths. It's a sign of superb humanity and love but, sadly, won't get the job done in combat. The battalion commander, angry and frustrated, relieves the company commander of his duties. Taking control himself, he soon neutralizes the enemy machine guns, losing few men in the process, and the assault regains momentum. The deposed officer observes it all with bemusement: it wasn't that bad. He just couldn't do it. In many ways, Rick Wagoner was that captain.

A question for the reader: whom would you rather serve under—the compassionate captain, or the ambitious, loud, somewhat brutal battalion commander? A magnificent human being, Rick was simply too nice, too introspective, and too thoughtful in many of his actions to see the company through the turbulence of 2008–09.

I should add that, without the subprime mortgage meltdown and the spike of gas prices to over $4.25, resulting in every company's sales volume dropping by over 50 percent, GM had every element in place for survival and growth through 2013. There was even a plan to weather a "normal" recession; this one wasn't normal. And the extremely well-received cars and trucks GM has rolled out in the past few years, including the new trio of small Chevrolets—Sonic, Cruze, and Spark—as well as the revolutionary Volt, were all conceived under Rick Wagoner's watch as CEO. The general media, unencumbered with any knowledge of automotive lead times, ascribes these to the new, Obama-picked board and executive group. I know better!

Rick Wagoner was the perfect "peacetime" CEO. His strategy was impeccable and he should have been more successful, but bad timing, bad luck, and the weight of still-unexpurgated GM costs and cultural traits proved his undoing.

I hated to see him go.

EPILOGUE

LEADERS, GOOD and bad.

What makes them tick?

A leader is a person who can create change and bring about a new state that, in his or her conviction, is superior. (I could, but won't, at length delve into negative leadership, where individuals, possessed of great leadership traits, use these to evil ends. Adolf Hitler and Joseph Stalin come to mind, but history and contemporary society have known many others.)

A leader usually possesses the ability, by the spoken or written word, to convince others of the soundness of his or her reasoning, thus enlisting their service in pursuit of the goal. Some leaders are exceptional in this area, demonstrating an oratorical style, a choice of words, and a speaking rhythm that is close to being hypnotic. President Barack Obama comes to mind, and even his most devoted fans will have to admit that the substance of his words often falls short of the soaring oratory. Leadership is definitely enhanced by the emotional component; followers can be so enraptured by a skilled, manipulative demagogue that they will place their own sense of critical judgment on hold and do anything the leader asks, unquestioningly. As with any leadership trait (for effective leadership is like a delicate prescription—a skillful blend of many ingredients, changing with time and circumstances as needed), the ability to sway, convince, and commit can be taken to dangerous extremes. A warning sign should read "Beware of the Messiah," but it would be useless: a good percentage of people fall under the speaker's thrall and are happy to have someone else guide their destiny.

Skill in the content and delivery of the spoken and written word is important to the successful leader if for no other reason than that, without it, he or she couldn't become a leader in the first place. Witness our political leader selection process, the most important element of which is "How does he/she look and sound on TV?"

The sine qua non for the positive, effective leader, one who genuinely advances a good cause, is integrity. It's what distinguishes the good, honorable leader from the manipulative maniacs who, while moving mountains, will move the wrong mountain to the wrong place for the wrong reasons. Integrity means, first of all, strict adherence to rules, regulations, laws, and the unwritten ethics of a particular field of endeavor. It means being evenhanded, not playing favorites among subordinates, and not trying to consolidate power by inciting one group of subordinates against another through the divide-and-conquer method. Integrity also requires a high degree of intellectual honesty and a consistent clarity of the core message: winning with integrity. Phrases like "We're not supposed to do this, but I doubt anyone will find out, so here's my plan" will not cross the lips of the leader who possesses integrity.

Truthfulness is part of integrity, and this is where it gets complicated. In order for a leader to reach the goal he or she is assigned to reach, it may be counterproductive, even harmful in the competitive sense, to blurt out the whole truth at every juncture. The effective leader knows the importance of confidentiality, practices it on a daily basis, and expects it of subordinates. But there is a huge difference between deflecting overly intrusive questioning with phrases like "I can't comment on that at this time; we'll tell you more later" and out-and-out lying or deliberate issuance of misleading information. Sadly, not all persons of high integrity are successful leaders, nor do all high-ranking leaders possess sufficient integrity, as the reader will by now have learned.

Courage is a basic cornerstone of good leadership. As stated earlier, leaders drive change and create a new reality, and that is never without risk. The battlefield leader has to seize the hill or fortification. This usually involves risk of serious wounds or death. The effective combat leader hides his own fear and displays the calm confidence that will make his subordinates perform at their optimum level. In the civilian world, the "risks" are there as well, but the consequences are less dire: failure could cost the leader reputation, trust, a bonus, even the job. The good leader assesses the risk and, once convinced that the goal is worth it, proceeds with dispatch. And here is where many "nominal" or "positional" leaders (those who enjoy leadership status by placement, but who don't possess the tools) will fail: they will spend so much time and energy identifying and minimizing risk that the assault against the objective is never launched. Corporations have many "positional" leaders. Successful entrepreneurs have none. They recognize the universal truth of "no risk, no reward."

Most (but not all) successful leaders possess a certain style. Tall or short, handsome or less so, natural leaders possess an innate quality (enhanced by experience and training, to be sure) we call "charisma." It's one of those things we can feel and experience yet find hard to describe, but those who possess it can literally enter a crowded room and, without bravado, fanfare, or other artificial means, be almost instantly noticed. President Charles de Gaulle of France was such a person. Of imposing physical stature, to be sure, he possessed a sense of posture, grooming, pace, bearing, speed or slowness of movement and response (depending on the situation) that made him literally "fill a room" by himself. The military looks for this in its officers; it's called "command presence." But it does not have to be defined in military terms. Albert Einstein had it, shaggy and poorly dressed as he was. President Ronald Reagan had the mystical aura, but the military rectitude, in his case, was replaced by a warm, affable, but intelligent and businesslike demeanor. The late Roger Smith, a former chairman and CEO of GM who oversaw one of its worst periods, was a nominal leader who, florid-faced, short in stature, and negatively gifted with a high-pitched squeaky voice, was definitely challenged in the department of charisma and command presence. Yet he led forcefully, took massive risks (not all of them intelligent), was intolerant of the opinions of others (a dangerous failing), and is generally credited with the overspending that set GM on the road to decline.

Can command presence, the look of leadership, be learned? Generally, yes. The Marine Corps and the military in general (with varying degrees of focus) insist on it. A straight, self-confident (not arrogant) posture, a steady walk, a calm expression, eyes that neither stare helplessly nor dart about but instead calmly sweep over the surroundings, scanning and assessing the situation, are all ingredients. They are enhanced by eye contact when conversing, a steady voice, and a manifest, mature sense of humor. Sadly, the nation's business schools teach none of this, preferring to convey "techniques" and "tools" rather than even the most elementary aspects of leadership behavior.

An effective leader is also tough—not necessarily physically, although that, too, helps bear the emotional and sometimes bodily stress that comes with leadership. The task is usually not easy, and resistance is a normal obstacle encountered when trying to change the status quo. Toughness implies the maintenance of a certain standard of behavior and discipline as demanded from subordinates. Casual humor and joking are fine, but the leader cannot become "pals" with his team members. He or she is in charge; he or she bears the responsibility and is accountable for results. The tough leader knows how to strike the right balance: never cruel, never unduly harsh, never "making them jump" to show who's boss, just relentlessly demanding and driving toward the goal with more energy and stamina than the subordinates expect.

Toughness is also accompanied by two related qualities:

consistency and focus. A good leader should be predictable in his or her reactions, demonstrating an expected set of behaviors under similar circumstances.

A mercurial nature is not a good leadership trait. Those being led need to sense a steady hand at the wheel, not one that yanks right or left with reckless abandon. Sure, course corrections are often necessary and have to be accomplished, but that's best done when accompanied by reasoned explanation to those being led as to just why the direction is being changed.

And nothing is harder for people to follow than a leader whose priorities constantly shift, where one day it's "defend market share at all cost" and the next day it's "reduce marketing expense, improve margins; we've got to make the profit forecast." Sure, a certain amount of bobbing and weaving—call it tactical maneuvering—is always required, but the core strategic priorities, the "what I want this organization to be, to stand for," can't change. With Rick Wagoner, it was the consistent thrust, the growth of the Chinese operation, a huge source of GM prosperity today. With Phil Caldwell, the unchanging strategic priority was quality and reliability. In my case, it was product excellence, an unwavering commitment to vehicles that customers would actually desire rather than be willing to settle for.

Leadership style and method (not long-term goals or strategic priorities) need to be "situational." A good leader has a portfolio of styles at his or her command, as the situation may dictate. There are times when absolute command and control are essential: we call them "crises." Whether in combat or in business, time is always of the essence. There is no time for "I think/you think." The leader must decide; the troops must obey. There are leaders who know only this style. They are successful "crisis managers" who know how to cut, slash, and burn without remorse or hesitation. They are often near useless in noncrisis situations, where the thoughtful leader solicits input from others, thus drawing on the collective intelligence of the organization. Yet too many so-called leaders are so comfortable with the cozy security blanket of collective, shared decisions that they are unable to call the shots. They desperately hope someone else will do it for them. Large corporations breed a lot of those; compromising, listening, sharing, avoiding mistakes is what got them to the top in the first place. The multistyle or multifaceted leader, like a good actor, can be participative, friendly, sharing, and humorous in the normal course of business. He or she can and must, however, be unflinching and stubborn if the situation calls for it. And anger, real or feigned, is an appropriate emotion when those accountable have failed. The good golfer has many clubs in his bag, and knows how to hit all of them, just as strong leaders have many styles to use as needed.

Many exceptional leaders are creative, with an innate ability to envisage a new state of affairs, a new reality. They can see the future with such clarity that they can describe it to others, thus enlisting them on the journey. The creative leader's mind can often come up with new, untried solutions when the team effort is mired in the solidifying concrete of obstacles, foreseen and unforeseen, and in the ever-present, grinding resistance of the dark forces who cling to the status quo. Creativity in leaders is nice to have;

many successful leaders are not creative. The other qualities of toughness, integrity, consistency, etc., are the real essentials. But the noncreative, analytically focused leader must recognize and accept that change, risk, new solutions, experiments, and "why don't we . . . ?" are necessary and must be fostered.

Since all leaders have some blend of the characteristics listed here, with none possessing all (nobody has a perfect score, due to human frailty and variability), the final judgment of a leader's quality must be results over time. The reason for the words "over time" is that, especially in large corporations with rapid changes in personnel assignments, a person can "luck out" by being placed in an impossible-to-fail position prepared by his or her predecessor. That leader, in the one- or two-year tenure, can deliver spectacular results not of his or her doing. This is "enhanced" when that leader is adept at taking credit for accomplishments with which he or she had little or nothing to do. I've seen these "ninety-day wonders" skillfully move from job to job, the situation coming up aces two or three times in a row. I obviously got to know a number of these from the inside and was shocked at their priority of "leadership credit" versus actual "leadership performance." Yet these people, darlings of senior management though they might have been, frequently ran aground and sank when they faced a new, unstructured, and difficult situation that they had to deal with themselves. Fancy business school buzzwords couldn't help out: they had to perform! And frequently, they did not. But a leader who consistently delivers, keeps promises, achieves success in many assignments and perhaps in a variety of cultures is a truly gifted and effective leader.

At the end of the day, delivering results should always be a leader's goal. In academia, it's quality of the students and reputation of the institution. In the military, it's battlefield victory with no more losses than necessary. And in business, it's shareholder value, brought about by profitability, market share growth, corporate reputation, and long-term outlook. In our still largely private enterprise system, shareholder value is the driver. We need more leaders who deliver it.

ACKNOWLEDGMENTS

THE AUTHOR would like to acknowledge and thank the numerous contributors to this work. As usual, my faithful administrative assistant, Amy King, did a lot of the leg work, copying, printing, sending, and following up.

Nancy Breedlove, a retired GM adminstrative assistant, once again translated my cursive handwritten document into correct type for the publisher. Thus, she became the first reader of "I+I," and her feedback was invaluable. She contributed more than one valid editorial suggestion.

As in the case of *Car Guys*, my editor, date-and-data researcher, and fact checker was the talented and hardworking John Cortez, who knows when he sees "too much," and skillfully takes it out.

Then there is Dee Allen, faithful adviser and publicist, as well as the crew at Portfolio, solid professionals with a sense of humor who make the publishing process relatively painless.

I thank them all for their support.

APPENDIX

SINCE THE business world likes quantification, with even the subjective, qualitative, and emotional reduced to a handy (if often misleading) set of numbers, I have attempted to craft a brief overview of each of the subjects examined in this book. The leadership traits evaluated are the ones I personally believe are the most important, and the weighting for each trait, from zero to ten, is also the product of my opinion and judgment. The reader may well have other views on traits and weighting. I have included some handy blank evaluation schedules on pages 217–219; you are invited to use them for leaders under whom you are proudly serving or pathetically suffering. You may wish to evaluate yourself or ask your subordinates to do so.

Those readers who have served under me may wish to do an evaluation of the author. It's never too late in one's career or life to receive some beneficial feedback, positive being preferred, but negative also accepted with gratitude!

GEORGES-ANDRÉ CHEVALLAZ

Scholar, military officer, easily elected president of his country. A charismatic, supremely intelligent, natural leader.

	GRADE 1–5	WEIGHT 1–10	SCORE
Integrity Character, honesty, trust	5	10	50
Courage Willing to take personal risk, be "unpopular"; does not turn tail in adversity	5	7	35
Style Bearing, charisma, command presence	5	5	25
Communication Skill Ability to influence others through spoken and written word	5	5	25
Toughness Holds people accountable; tackles low performers	5	6	30
Adaptability Ability to adjust to changing environment; modifies approach as needed	4	6	24
Consistency and Focus No "buzzword" or "initiative of the week"	4	5	20
Sense of Priority Unwavering commitment to key strategic goals	5	8	40
Creativity Inventive, imaginative; able to see new approaches and solutions	5	7	35
Results The "bottom line" over time; consistently delivers what was committed to	5	10	50
Total	48		334

STAFF SERGEANT DONALD GIUSTO

Tough, unflinching; a combat-hardened professional Marine. Through his tireless efforts, thousands of callow civilian youths from all walks of life were turned into members of the world's finest fighting force.

	GRADE 1–5	WEIGHT 1–10	SCORE
Integrity Character, honesty, trust	5	10	50
Courage Willing to take personal risk, be "unpopular"; does not turn tail in adversity	5	7	35
Style Bearing, charisma, command presence	5	5	25
Communication Skill Ability to influence others through spoken and written word	4	5	20
Toughness Holds people accountable; tackles low performers	5	6	30
Adaptability Ability to adjust to changing environment; modifies approach as needed	2	6	12
Consistency and Focus No "buzzword" or "initiative of the week"	4	5	20
Sense of Priority Unwavering commitment to key strategic goals	5	8	40
Creativity Inventive, imaginative; able to see new approaches and solutions	1	7	7
Results The "bottom line" over time; consistently delivers what was committed to	5	10	50
Total	41		289

ROBERT "BOB" WACHTLER

Uncouth, unpolished, of modest education, he knew the GM system and how to bend it to his powerful will. (He would **not** thrive in today's humorless "politically correct" environment.)

	GRADE 1–5	WEIGHT 1–10	SCORE
Integrity Character, honesty, trust	4	10	40
Courage Willing to take personal risk, be "unpopular"; does not turn tail in adversity	5	7	35
Style Bearing, charisma, command presence	3	5	15
Communication Skill Ability to influence others through spoken and written word	3	5	15
Toughness Holds people accountable; tackles low performers	5	6	30
Adaptability Ability to adjust to changing environment; modifies approach as needed	1	6	6
Consistency and Focus No "buzzword" or "initiative of the week"	4	5	20
Sense of Priority Unwavering commitment to key strategic goals	4	8	32
Creativity Inventive, imaginative; able to see new approaches and solutions	1	7	7
Results The "bottom line" over time; consistently delivers what was committed to	4	10	40
Total	34		240

RALPH MASON

A large man with several degrees from the school of hard knocks. A cheerful (but serious) alcoholic. Ralph nevertheless focused on what was important and advanced the cause of GM and its shareholders.

	GRADE 1–5	WEIGHT 1–10	SCORE
Integrity Character, honesty, trust	4	10	40
Courage Willing to take personal risk, be "unpopular"; does not turn tail in adversity	3	7	21
Style Bearing, charisma, command presence	3	5	15
Communication Skill Ability to influence others through spoken and written word	3	5	15
Toughness Holds people accountable; tackles low performers	2	6	12
Adaptability Ability to adjust to changing environment; modifies approach as needed	2	6	12
Consistency and Focus No "buzzword" or "initiative of the week"	3	5	15
Sense of Priority Unwavering commitment to key strategic goals	3	8	24
Creativity Inventive, imaginative; able to see new approaches and solutions	2	7	14
Results The "bottom line" over time; consistently delivers what was committed to	4	10	40
Total	29		208

EBERHARD VON KUENHEIM

Of aristocratic origin, the baron nevertheless could and did get his hands dirty to get the job done. Not always delightful to work under, he became the longest-serving automotive CEO in history, transforming BMW from a tiny, regional auto company into a global luxury-car powerhouse.

	GRADE 1–5	WEIGHT 1–10	SCORE
Integrity Character, honesty, trust	4	10	40
Courage Willing to take personal risk, be "unpopular"; does not turn tail in adversity	4	7	28
Style Bearing, charisma, command presence	4	5	20
Communication Skill Ability to influence others through spoken and written word	5	5	25
Toughness Holds people accountable; tackles low performers	5	6	30
Adaptability Ability to adjust to changing environment; modifies approach as needed	3	6	18
Consistency and Focus No "buzzword" or "initiative of the week"	5	5	25
Sense of Priority Unwavering commitment to key strategic goals	5	8	40
Creativity Inventive, imaginative; able to see new approaches and solutions	3	7	21
Results The "bottom line" over time; consistently delivers what was committed to	5	10	50
Total	43		297

PHILIP CALDWELL

The teetotaler who would not even touch such "stimulants" as tea and coffee. Almost totally deprived of even the slightest sense of humor, he also exhibited a bizarre fondness for company-supplied "perks." Still, hard to like as he may have been, he gained respect for his persistent focus on quality and product excellence.

	GRADE 1–5	WEIGHT 1–10	SCORE
Integrity Character, honesty, trust	3	10	30
Courage Willing to take personal risk, be "unpopular"; does not turn tail in adversity	3	7	21
Style Bearing, charisma, command presence	4	5	20
Communication Skill Ability to influence others through spoken and written word	3	5	15
Toughness Holds people accountable; tackles low performers	4	6	24
Adaptability Ability to adjust to changing environment; modifies approach as needed	2	6	12
Consistency and Focus No "buzzword" or "initiative of the week"	5	5	25
Sense of Priority Unwavering commitment to key strategic goals	5	8	40
Creativity Inventive, imaginative; able to see new approaches and solutions	2	7	14
Results The "bottom line" over time; consistently delivers what was committed to	4	10	40
Total	35		241

HAROLD A. "RED" POLING

Tough, opinionated, uncompromising, often blind to the qualities and inputs from others, he was of the school that held "if you can't measure it, it doesn't exist." Serving under him was like going through Marine boot camp all over again. I learned from the best, who could also be the worst. All in all, a successful leader.

	GRADE 1–5	WEIGHT 1–10	SCORE
Integrity Character, honesty, trust	4	10	40
Courage Willing to take personal risk, be "unpopular"; does not turn tail in adversity	5	7	35
Style Bearing, charisma, command presence	3	5	15
Communication Skill Ability to influence others through spoken and written word	3	5	15
Toughness Holds people accountable; tackles low performers	5	6	30
Adaptability Ability to adjust to changing environment; modifies approach as needed	2	6	12
Consistency and Focus No "buzzword" or "initiative of the week"	4	5	20
Sense of Priority Unwavering commitment to key strategic goals	5	8	40
Creativity Inventive, imaginative; able to see new approaches and solutions	2	7	14
Results The "bottom line" over time; consistently delivers what was committed to	5	10	50
Total	38		271

LEE IACOCCA

Surely one of the most powerful, charismatic, and successful leaders in American industrial history, he was not without a profound, but cleverly concealed, sense of insecurity. Action-oriented, motivational, focused, he possessed skills that were such that I later often found myself saying "This wouldn't be happening if Iacocca were at the helm."

	GRADE 1–5	WEIGHT 1–10	SCORE
Integrity Character, honesty, trust	4	10	40
Courage Willing to take personal risk, be "unpopular"; does not turn tail in adversity	5	7	35
Style Bearing, charisma, command presence	5	5	25
Communication Skill Ability to influence others through spoken and written word	5	5	25
Toughness Holds people accountable; tackles low performers	5	6	30
Adaptability Ability to adjust to changing environment; modifies approach as needed	3	6	18
Consistency and Focus No "buzzword" or "initiative of the week"	3	5	15
Sense of Priority Unwavering commitment to key strategic goals	4	8	32
Creativity Inventive, imaginative; able to see new approaches and solutions	5	7	35
Results The "bottom line" over time; consistently delivers what was committed to	5	10	50
Total	44		305

ROBERT J. "BOB" EATON

A GM "lifer" who became CEO of Chrysler. A gentle leader of modest charisma and command presence, he was an immensely supportive partner to me when I served him as president. Although badly outmaneuvered by the wily Germans in the ill-fated "merger of equals" with Daimler, he nevertheless made many shareholders very wealthy. And that's what CEOs are supposed to do.

	GRADE 1–5	WEIGHT 1–10	SCORE
Integrity Character, honesty, trust	4	10	40
Courage Willing to take personal risk, be "unpopular"; does not turn tail in adversity	3	7	21
Style Bearing, charisma, command presence	3	5	15
Communication Skill Ability to influence others through spoken and written word	3	5	15
Toughness Holds people accountable; tackles low performers	2	6	12
Adaptability Ability to adjust to changing environment; modifies approach as needed	3	6	18
Consistency and Focus No "buzzword" or "initiative of the week"	4	5	20
Sense of Priority Unwavering commitment to key strategic goals	3	8	24
Creativity Inventive, imaginative; able to see new approaches and solutions	2	7	14
Results The "bottom line" over time; consistently delivers what was committed to	5	10	50
Total	32		229

ARTHUR M. HAWKINS

It's hard to say any nice things about Art, a sometime "man of the cloth" with a badly bent moral compass. Although CEO of a midsized ($2.5 billion) company, Exide Technologies, he was a pioneer in one area: his indictment and conviction came years ahead of that of the later, much-publicized fraudulent leaderships of companies like Enron and others.

	GRADE 1–5	WEIGHT 1–10	SCORE
Integrity Character, honesty, trust	1	10	10
Courage Willing to take personal risk, be "unpopular"; does not turn tail in adversity	2	7	14
Style Bearing, charisma, command presence	4	5	20
Communication Skill Ability to influence others through spoken and written word	4	5	20
Toughness Holds people accountable; tackles low performers	4	6	24
Adaptability Ability to adjust to changing environment; modifies approach as needed	2	6	12
Consistency and Focus No "buzzword" or "initiative of the week"	1	5	5
Sense of Priority Unwavering commitment to key strategic goals	1	8	8
Creativity Inventive, imaginative; able to see new approaches and solutions	1	7	7
Results The "bottom line" over time; consistently delivers what was committed to	1	10	10
Total	21		130

G. RICHARD "RICK" WAGONER

By education, background, temperament, and physical stature, an almost ideal CEO. A proponent of a new, more nimble GM and the architect of GM's crucially important entry into China, Rick's gentility, sense of fairness, and compassion prevented him from acting with the necessary speed and ruthlessness when the ultimately fatal storm clouds gathered. Those who malign him fail to comprehend all the good he did.

	GRADE 1–5	WEIGHT 1–10	SCORE
Integrity Character, honesty, trust	5	10	50
Courage Willing to take personal risk, be "unpopular"; does not turn tail in adversity	3	7	21
Style Bearing, charisma, command presence	5	5	25
Communication Skill Ability to influence others through spoken and written word	4	5	20
Toughness Holds people accountable; tackles low performers	2	6	12
Adaptability Ability to adjust to changing environment; modifies approach as needed	3	6	18
Consistency and Focus No "buzzword" or "initiative of the week"	2	5	10
Sense of Priority Unwavering commitment to key strategic goals	4	8	32
Creativity Inventive, imaginative; able to see new approaches and solutions	3	7	21
Results The "bottom line" over time; consistently delivers what was committed to	3	10	30
Total	34		239

APPENDIX

	GRADE 1–5	WEIGHT 1–10	SCORE
Integrity Character, honesty, trust			
Courage Willing to take personal risk, be "unpopular"; does not turn tail in adversity			
Style Bearing, charisma, command presence			
Communication Skill Ability to influence others through spoken and written word			
Toughness Holds people accountable; tackles low performers			
Adaptability Ability to adjust to changing environment; modifies approach as needed			
Consistency and Focus No "buzzword" or "initiative of the wook"			
Sense of Priority Unwavering commitment to key strategic goals			
Creativity Inventive, imaginative; able to see new approaches and solutions			
Results The "bottom line" over time; consistently delivers what was committed to			
Total			

	GRADE 1–5	WEIGHT 1–10	SCORE
Integrity Character, honesty, trust			
Courage Willing to take personal risk, be "unpopular"; does not turn tail in adversity			
Style Bearing, charisma, command presence			
Communication Skill Ability to influence others through spoken and written word			
Toughness Holds people accountable; tackles low performers			
Adaptability Ability to adjust to changing environment; modifies approach as needed			
Consistency and Focus No "buzzword" or "initiative of the week"			
Sense of Priority Unwavering commitment to key strategic goals			
Creativity Inventive, imaginative; able to see new approaches and solutions			
Results The "bottom line" over time; consistently delivers what was committed to			
Total			

	GRADE 1–5	WEIGHT 1–10	SCORE
Integrity Character, honesty, trust			
Courage Willing to take personal risk, be "unpopular"; does not turn tail in adversity			
Style Bearing, charisma, command presence			
Communication Skill Ability to influence others through spoken and written word			
Toughness Holds people accountable; tackles low performers			
Adaptability Ability to adjust to changing environment; modifies approach as needed			
Consistency and Focus No "buzzword" or "initiative of the week"			
Sense of Priority Unwavering commitment to key strategic goals			
Creativity Inventive, imaginative; able to see new approaches and solutions			
Results The "bottom line" over time; consistently delivers what was committed to			
Total			

INDEX